LOVE,
UNPACKED

First paperback edition May 2020

Book design by Dania Zafar

ISBN 978-1-7346120-0-4 (paperback)
ISBN 978-1-7346120-1-1 (hardcover)
ISBN 978-1-7346120-2-8 (ebook)

Published by Jan & Lucy Press
www.andifranklin.com

LOVE, UNPACKED

DUMP OUT YOUR BAG AND STEP INTO
THE LOVE YOU'VE BEEN SEARCHING FOR

ANDI FRANKLIN

*For the women who have been looking for love
in all the wrong places, this one is for you.*

CONTENTS

INTRODUCTION

"No woman gets an orgasm from shining the kitchen floor."

— BETTY FRIEDAN

I HATE THE INTRODUCTION OF A BOOK AS MUCH AS I DESPISE spiders, but here I am creepy crawling my way on to this front page, hoping to grab your attention long enough to get picked up, put in your bag to take home, and examine more closely. *Don't read this as a sudden empathetic breakthrough for spiders on my part. I'll scream and chase them like the deranged chef in "The Little Mermaid" going after Sebastian, every single time.* The stress of writing an introduction is like getting picked for teams in middle school P.E. class. I picture all of us authors in our matching cotton gym shorts trying to puff our chests and look taller, waiting for you, the reader, to decide who gets picked first. You're careful, of course. You won't choose just anyone to grace your bookshelves, and we respect that about you; in turn, we spend hours agonizing over getting this opening pitch just right, so that our value will be undeniable and you'll have no choice but to recognize what an asset we'll be to your literary team.

Your time is precious. You probably only have about five more seconds before your toddler starts trying to eat something off the floor. Or you have to hurry home before your spouse sees all of the late-night Amazon purchases you made two days ago, so I'll cut right to the chase: This book is about sex, not in a *Fifty Shades of Grey* kind of way, more like one of the inevitable soul-reaching conversations that happen when you invite your best girlfriend over to do face masks and watch RomComs all night. We're going to laugh, cry, and cringe together. Maybe we'll throw a little popcorn at the book at specific points and laugh too loud over a couple punch lines that we'll have to go back and reread. Pee breaks are optional, wine is suggested, and an open heart is of the upmost importance.

If you allow me, I want to take you through my journey of self-discovery to understand how I'd gotten to a point in my life where I was deeply in love with the man of my dreams, but I still couldn't be vulnerable with him in the bedroom. Yes, this book is about sex, but sex itself goes so much deeper than bed-rocking; and when I began diving into my own issues with intimacy, I uncovered staggering truths about myself that I'd long kept tucked away. Too often we look at our problems as one dimensional, but everything within us is connected. I thought my issue was sexual, but what I found was actually a collection of unchecked trauma that was manifesting itself as something else. A wolf in sheep's clothing was living within the walls of my heart.

In the spirit of transparency, I'll come right out the gate and tell you on stationary, I'm about as impressive as a box of Dots in your kid's Halloween candy. I barely graduated high school (a story for later), never monetized my blog, and I spend the greater portion of my days cleaning up after my family and writing—which to everyone else means I actually just watch reruns of "Fixer Upper" all day and try to make myself seem more relevant by claiming the title of a "writer" over that of a "housewife."

"What do you do?" actually means "how do you make money?" and well, I don't. But I'm mega successful in love and sex. You can see how that's not the kind of success I lead with when introducing myself at a dinner party.

"So what do you do?"
"Me? I'm highly successful in the field of love and sex."
"Fascinating. Are you a therapist?"
"No, no. I'm just really good at embracing my sexuality and loving myself for who I was always meant to be. An expert, really."

Now, I wouldn't say I'm an expert in the traditional sense or definition. My flexibility is that of a T-Rex, so there are no legs over the head or body pretzels happening in our bed. And don't ask me about my favorite toys because like I tell my husband all of the time, *I'm in the moment man, so I don't have space to take mental notes on the pluses and minuses of each dildo, vibrator, and plug that comes my way.* Like I said, I'm not an expert in the literal sense. It's more like the "My husband and I found what works for us and we regularly engage without embarrassment or shame" kind of way. To some that may not seem like something to feel successful about, but it's the sort of feat I want to shout from the rooftops because the road to get where I am now was covered in layers of trauma, pain, and suppression. I used to avoid orgasms like the swimsuit aisle. I didn't realize it at the time, but my past was keeping me a prisoner from my most basic human right—to give love and be loved—for my entire life.

If life is a grand adventure, then the triumphs and tragedies we experience are tokens of wisdom that we can either use or tuck away out of fear. I never considered how a suitcase full of baggage, collected over my lifetime, could be overflowing into my relationships until one morning, when my husband casually said four little words that rocked my world and catapulted me into a full-blown makeover of the mind, body, and soul. Each chapter in this book shares a lesson I had to unpack from my past, so I could step into the love I'd searched for my entire life. We all know our own stories; we've lived, spoken, and replayed them over and over, but we don't usually spend much time examining what they mean in the bigger picture or how they seep into other areas of our lives. It's only when we take the time to unpack these silenced souvenirs collected throughout our lifetimes that we can see the full spectrum of impact they've had on us. It takes grit and a willingness to look in the darkest corners of our bags in order to genuinely move forward, but the juice is worth the squeeze. You can't change the past, but you can sure as hell learn from it, if you're willing to open your eyes to the deeper meaning of each story you're white knuckling.

Honestly, I didn't backpack through the wilderness, travel the world, sell all of my belongings, join a nudist survival colony, or anything quite so dramatic. But who says you have to quit your life and start a new one to go on an epic adventure? The greatest quest of your existence lies in an overflowing bag at your feet, waiting for you to unlock its mysteries and treasures. My hope for you, dear reader, is that these pages filled with some of my most tender moments serve as an invitation for you to go through your own suitcase and find the love you've always longed to give and receive. Moreover, I'm inclined to remind you that this book is filled with my truth. While I've done my best to tell each story as accurately as possible, I'm also aware that my recollection of events may be different than the people who were involved because that's how perception works. I've changed several names in the spirit of privacy and respect for those I mention. Again, this is my story. I've tried to the best of my ability not to drag anyone through the mud. That being said, some of the characters on my road were easier to cover for than others. I hope that even in the moments that make you want to write an enraged series of tweets to them, or to me, that you can still find a slice of humanity within each person. Remember, someone out there could probably write a book about me, or you, with less than becoming narratives about us, too.

Now that we're officially done with formalities, let's kick off our shoes, grab some snacks, and get unpacking. I want to take you back to the start when one matter-of-fact statement from my husband sparked a challenge that would burst my bag wide open. This is a path of great resistance, lifelong resistance. It also embodies the road never before traveled, the most significant trip of my life without ever leaving home. And it all began with one glaring truth.

THE CHALLENGE: AIRLINES CHARGE EXTRA FOR BAGGAGE THIS HEAVY

"The greater the obstacle, the more glory in overcoming it."

— MOLIÈRE

"YOU NEVER INITIATE SEX."

My husband Derek is standing in his closet, slipping a powder blue button-up shirt back on its hanger when those four little words leave his lips. It feels like a dagger in the chest — kiss of death. It's a shot to the heart, and I'm apparently to blame. I thought everything was fine. No, great! Weren't we having great sex? Wasn't our sex life great?

"You never initiate sex" falls matter-of-factly out of his mouth, but what I hear is "you're a failure of a wife," and I'm ready to dig a ditch and toss my loser limbs into it.

I pipe back. *"What are you talking about? I do too! Just last week, on Wednesday!"*

The problem presents itself to me like a popped tastebud on my tongue as soon as the words leave my lips, but it's too late to go back now.

SHIELDS UP.

When I was younger, there was this magical place called "Lazerstar" in our small suburban town that was essentially the Holy Grail for children between the ages of 4-18. Think, laser tag meets arcade, meets snack bar sanctuary with a stale water smell that only comes from an undersized and overused air conditioning unit. Every inch of the place was covered in glow-in-the-dark space-themed wallpaper. The moment you stepped inside, an impressive display of prizes met your gaze. They had Cyclone, car racing, ski ball, and the dump truck game that I frequently made my bitch. Kids would crowd around the Mortal Kombat arcade machine, oohing and aahing and yelling, "Finish him!" as they watched epic battles between Scorpion and Lui Kang. The tickets and nacho cheese were ever-flowing, and every time I stepped inside those galaxy decorated walls, I silently declared that if Heaven didn't have a Lazerstar, I didn't want to party in those pearly gates.

The arcade boasted an impressive crowd with its flashing lights and victory bells, but it was a prerequisite for the tantalizing adrenaline rush of laser tag. Like fifteen minutes on the treadmill before a weight lifting session, the arcade served as a warmup before the big event. No amount of bonuses could hold a candle to seeing your hand-picked code name gracing the scoreboard for everyone to see. The focal point of the entire building was two modest black marquees above the laser room entrance, showing real-time scores and rankings for the teams playing inside. The highest scorer of each match received a free game, so the stakes were staggering. We all wanted to see our name in those red neon lights and to experience the surge of pride and glory as we walked through the laser room and back into the arcade among our new, adoring fans.

Thank you! Yes, I'm smurfitup55, and I know, I know, meeting your hero can be intimidating, but I'm just like everyone else, I promise, but only, with the highest score in the entire building, no big deal!

You could claim childhood fame in your game record, but like any battle, you still had to work as a team to be triumphant. Upon writing your chosen code name on a tiny slice of paper with a miniature pencil, they separated everyone into one of two sides: The green team and the red team. Each wave of players was broken up into unique missions, and they'd call out on the loudspeaker when it was your turn.

Mission: Alpha Delta Beta, line up!

This is where the arcade served its divine purpose. Games were a distraction from the sweaty palms and shaking legs of laser tag anticipation. When your mission was finally called, you'd assemble, about-face on your color-coded side and proceed to size up your competition standing across from you. Fighter stances, sly grins, and seemingly random laughter to cripple self-esteem were highly encouraged during this roll call. After they let you soak in the faces of your enemies in the light, a black door would open, and a part-time teenage employee with atti-tude would usher everyone into a small room with benches and colorful paint splatter on the walls, illuminated by black-lights. There, the referee (who was also a part-time teenage employee with attitude) would explain the rules and show you how to use your gun/vest combo: No running. No hitting. No drinking the blood of your foes, yada yada yada, before opening a door that led to a large, cold room with rows of green and red laser tag vests decorating the soft grey walls as far as the eye could see. The vests were heavier than anticipated, with a laser gun attached to a long cord coming smack dab out of the middle, and targets on your shoulders, back, and chest that looked like police car sirens. If you looked directly down on the breastplate, it lit up with your stats, showing you exactly how many points you'd accrued, so you could keep track during the game. The gun kept track of your "ammo" and once it began flashing "0" the gun would stop working until you went back to one of two charging stations to "fill up."

After snapping our vests into place, each team was instructed to follow its assigned color referee to opposite ends of the massive indoor arena. There, a pissed off prepubescent employee would show us how to charge our lasers at the charging stations and send us in one by one to load up before getting on the walkie talkie and signaling "go time." Once everyone on each team was juiced up, an eruption of music fit for Rocky Balboa would fill the room and a voice on the speaker would declare, "GAME ON."

Glow tape acted as a guiding light to find your way around the tall, gym mat pillars within the course. It was steal the flag style; only the flag was these giant cyclone targets on each team's home base. I'm supremely competitive, which is the polite way to say, "I'm not here to play; I'm here to bloody effin' win!" Each game felt like the most significant battle of my life, and I had a complete strategy in place on how to get the most points and see my name at the tippy top of those black marquees. Most people spent their time shooting the opposite team, but that's because they were damn fools who didn't have long enough attention spans to listen to the rules in the beginning. But me? I had my eyes on the prize. You gained the most points by hitting the targets, so I'd creep through the course as quickly and stealthily as possible and make my way into a little unknown nook where I could reach the targets with my laser beams. I'd perch up in my hidden corner and use every single bullet I had for those targets until my gun read "0," and it was time to recharge. Then, I'd speed walk back to base with my arms up (the universal signal of "don't waste your lasers on me because it won't count"), load up, and go again.

I was a total master of my craft, the Lara Croft of laser beams. Yet since I'm a mere mortal, every so often, I found myself caught in the opposing team's crossfire. Getting shot was the pits because your gun would disable, and then a Darth Vader voice would interrupt all of your plans for total domination and force you to stand there exposed and defenseless until it finished shouting four foul words:

"Shields up! Shields down."

The moment my shields went up, my guard would, too. It had to since my vest would announce to everyone within ear range that I was around and vulnerable. Those words took a million years to finish, and I'd be forced into paralysis while I waited, unable to use my trigger finger and often left to the harassment of some annoying little kid who didn't understand Laser tag etiquette and was hell-bent on reshooting me the moment my shields dropped. *Stop following me! I'm disabled! Get out of here, little kid! You're ruining my plan!*

Spending so much time in my particular corner of the course always left me feeling invincible, until of course, I wasn't. I really had no choice but to learn and master the sacred art of resting bitch face to deter overbearing peers and foes from following me back to base to attack the moment my vest stopped singing, and gun reloaded. The thirty seconds it took for my vest to shut up were agonizing. All the blood from my fingertips would rush to my face, and I'd start to get the panic sweats where you could practically smell Dr. Pepper oozing out of my pores. Laser tag wasn't a game for me; it was an expression of my skillset as a human being, and I couldn't let some kid with nacho cheese stains all over his pants beat me. The idea of that alone was enough to send my racing heart into cardiac arrest. Once that robotic male voice declared shields down, the soda sweats would subside, blood would evenly distribute through my body again, and I'd slide right back into the zone, ready to execute my master plan, and hope to avoid another run-in with those four foul words.

Now I was focused on a new set of words as dead air lingered between Derek and me. Last Wednesday. I can pinpoint the exact day I initiated sex, and it was a week ago. Before that? Probably a month, as in, thirty to thirty-one days (unless you count that rebel, February). We have sex every day, but I can only remember 1-2 instances in a month's span where I actually initiated.

SHIELDS DOWN.

Damn it. See, here's my problem, and it's a big one: I don't like to be wrong. I've already said out loud that I do initiate sex, and now I'm stuck trying to convince my husband—who isn't an idiot and has been keeping mental tabs of when I'm getting after him—that his memory is wrong. That I'm actually the instigating sex goddess I claim to be, because this is something insecure people do when they feel attacked or taken off-guard.

SHIELDS UP.

I don't initiate sex?! There goes that Franklin memory again! You don't remember uh, two weeks ago when I, uh, grabbed you while we were watching TV? And then, yeah, I definitely released my inner beast at least three more times that week. I never get any credit around here thanks to that shit memory of yours.

He shrugs me off quickly. He knows when I'm trying to trap him. Annoyed but also used to my shenanigans, he lets out a breathy "heh" before walking out of the room, leaving me alone with the weight of his words. His truth.

SHIELDS DOWN.

I never initiate sex.

You know the feeling you get when you've been walking around all day with a piece of spinach in your teeth, and not a single person informs you about it? That's how this revelation felt. I was downright embarrassed and also annoyed because, *Why in the hell have you let me walk around this long with the damn spinach in-between my canines?* It's entirely possible to have a happy marriage with substantial sex and also be utterly blind to your shortcomings in apparent happy marriage with significant sex.

Initiating sex doesn't come naturally to me. It's not because I don't want sex.
I want sex.
I crave it.
I enjoy it.
I need it.

Still, years of believing it was wrong to be a sexual creature cling to me. They're like an oil stain on a dark wash tee. You can't really see it unless you're in direct sunlight, but it's still there. I stood with the sun beaming down on me, and the marks were clear.

You're vile. You're sinful. You're unworthy. You never initiate sex because you don't deserve passion and love and full-body acceptance.

My inner voice is a real bitch with an uncanny ability to string endless tall tales about my inadequacies from the tinniest comments. She weaves stories of abandonment and infidelity if Derek is running fifteen minutes late from work, so you can imagine the field day she had with a confrontation like this one: *You don't initiate sex, girlfriend! Why would he want to be with someone as insecure and boring as you? You can't even fulfill his needs. You're a loser — a terrible wife. And you know, what? That outfit looks ridiculous on you!*

I wish I could tell you this sort of negative self-talk was a rare occurrence for me, but that would be a big fat lie. In truth, my habit of talking down on myself had been as natural as inhaling and exhaling for as long as I can remember. My knee jerk reaction when anyone within a 100-mile radius of me was unhappy was to blame myself, and I acquired a laundry list of possible reasons why I was just the worst, for all occasions.

So there he stands, being the open, honest, loving communicator every girl dreams of, and I'm pissed. Part of me wishes he would've just kept that mortifying comment to himself, and the other half knew doing so would've been a one-way ticket to an unhappy marriage. Nobody wants to look in the mirror and see wilted spinach staring back at them. Still, it's a hard pill to swallow, and it leaves an aftertaste that's almost worse than the fishy burps you get from taking your omega-3s. *Almost.*

You never initiate sex.

This is true. It's a fact, and now I'm being forced to take notice of my non-sex-initiating-skillset. So I pour a glass of wine and invite my alter-ego, Over-analyzer, to join me. She and I will spend the next 500 million hours digging deep into my psyche, unlocking secrets I buried long ago and a stockpile of baggage in a desperate attempt to answer a straightforward question: *How did I get here?*

Here, being the place where I'm a grown ass, adult woman who loves her husband, and sex, and intimacy, yet somehow cannot initiate sex. Days, weeks, and bottles of wine later, I finally came up with an answer that made sense. Even now—married to the love of my life, I was still looking for love in all the wrong places. I was tossing a freight train sized purse over my husband's shoulders filled with my value, worth, and confidence and expecting him to keep it handy for me whenever I needed to slip on something a little more comfortable.

Hey, babe. Can you grab my self-confidence really fast? Oh, and my lip balm. My soul and lips are both super chapped.

Of course I never initiated sex. That poor man was the unknowing keeper of all the things that would cue a person to act first. I was falling in line with what I thought he wanted 100% of the time, so if he didn't initiate intimacy because he was waiting for me to, you know, actually make him feel desired first, then I'd assume he was uninterested or tired or angry with me for something. And then, I'd ask him a million times if he was okay and go to bed confused as to what I'd done to ruin the romantic night when in all actuality it was what I *hadn't* done.

Marriage is fun.

UNPACKING: THE BAG

I'm going to be straight up with you: I didn't want to fix this "issue" at first. There, I said it. Don't get me wrong; I love my husband something fierce. He still gives me the tingles when the sun hits his face, and his eyes and lips illuminate. As I type this, I'm turning myself on just thinking about it, so I think you catch my drift. He's an eleven on a bad day, and I want to do bad things to that man all the freaking time. I just didn't want to initiate those sexy things.

You see, I'm a closer. You don't send your best closer in for the introductory meeting; they'd seem too desperate and ruin everything. No, your closer is best reserved for when the deal is already practically in the bag, and you need someone to tickle the balls a bit to land the deal. And that's me. That's where I shine. Closing and ball-tickling and trying not to come on too strong until I'm sure it's mine. See how I rationalize my position yet again? You guys, I'm really good at making an argument for myself in a pinch. It's a specialty of mine straight off the secret menu. *Can I get a large order of brainwashing yourself into believing you don't have any problems, with a side of crippling denial? Hold the self-loathing today; I'm trying to watch my figure.*

Maybe it was something in his voice that day or perhaps I was just tired of my shit? Once I fought off the urge to brush him aside and continue down my path as a predictable yet solid closer, I made a quiet decision to spend some serious time working on my inner self. It was time for a career change. Update the resume girl, because you're wanted in a position as an opener, an instigator, a let's-start-this-night-off-right-er. And deep, WAY DEEP down, I knew it was something I desperately craved for myself, too.

You never initiate sex.

Shields up. Shields down.

Challenge accepted.

The funny fact about challenges is that they're freakin' challenging. What? Were you expecting an Instagram worthy quote there? Sorry to disappoint, but the truth is that we all say we like a good challenge, but once we have to dive into a said challenge and get our hands dirty, we remember that we prefer our clean cuticles and powdered nails to the cracked, dirt-filled ones that come with the work. Someone sitting in front of a computer one day found a way to take the word "challenge" and turn it into glamour. He or she edited, filtered, and put it on an all-white marble countertop covered in dozens of fresh peonies and gold flaked coffee and the rest of us drooled over it like damn fools, admiring and gasping and declaring that we too, wanted a challenge if that's what challenges look like.

Only real challenges more accurately resemble a construction worker after pulling an 80-hour work week. They're tedious, sometimes dangerous, and almost always covered in layers of grime, blood, sweat, and tears. They wear hard hats, giant goggles, and boots for support and safety, rather than fashion. Challenges don't look like a beautiful blonde in Lululemons holding her glass water bottle and popping her booty out with the caption, "If you want it, work for it!" No, they're more akin to Ace Ventura running wildly with the white bat in tow, terrified and disgusted and just trying to get to the damn cage before the creature defecates all over the place.

When I said yes to Derek's challenge, I think a part of me was saying yes to Lululemon and manicured nails. Part of me was ready to give it my best-curated version of effort and spend more time talking about the challenge than actually working through it. But when I opened up the tattered bag I'd been forcing him to lug around for me and began rummaging through its chaotic contents, I realized the reason it was overflowing was because I'd never once in my life removed a single item from it. Sure, I'd found ways to condense, but only so I could fit more stuff inside its walls. It was a hoarder's paradise, so full of lifelong traumas, beliefs, insecurities, and everything in-between that I couldn't reach the bottom. Everything was still there, and I was just compacting it, so I'd have room for more. On the top sat my inability to initiate sex, but underneath it lied years of unchecked issues. I needed to Marie Kondo the hoarder hell that was my soul, stat. Sure, these events happened to me, but do they spark joy? If not, then it was time to thank them for our time together and kiss them goodbye.

If I were ever going to become an instigator, if I were ever going to have the opportunity to experience profound connection and vulnerability, I'd need to do far more than pull sexual confidence out of a hat. In reality, I'd need to unpack my bag completely. This meant that I had to put on my big girl panties and trade in those fancy leggings for some heavy-duty pants. This implied I'd need a hard hat, goggles, and a blueprint of everything

I needed to demolish, fix, and rebuild. So I laced up, bent down, and flipped my purse full of emotional chaos over dumping every last thing out onto the floor in front of me. I wanted to start from the beginning. I tried to find the first memory ever to make its way into this bag, so I combed through the petrified pile until I found it. There it was—the very first item to ever make its way into this purse of mine. A tattered, stained, crumpled up piece of paper. I pulled the edges apart to reveal its identity. A $25 Target gift certificate, addressed to a seven-year-old little girl. It was addressed to me.

ABANDONMENT: POLLY POCKET NEVER HAD TO DEAL WITH THIS SHIT

"The sun does not abandon the moon to darkness."

— BRIAN A. MCBRIDE

LONG AGO, IN THE YEAR 1994, THE EARTH WAS OVERRUN BY skorts, sparkly jelly shoes, and brightly colored snap clips. It was a trip around the sun full of notable drama, heartbreak, and triumph from Kurt Cobain's suicide, to O.J. Simpson's arrest, to the release of Disney's *The Lion King*. The denim on denim crime rate was at an all-time high and children everywhere were forced into the unthinkable torture of commercial breaks with no option to pause, rewind, or save their favorite Rugrats episode for later. I was but a girl on the cusp of her seventh birthday, not quite old enough for *"Are You Afraid Of The Dark?"* yet free to sing the verses of the number one Boyz II Men hit, *"I'll Make Love To You"* without so much as a blink from surrounding adults.

My parents had divorced a few years back, so we made our entire conveyer belt child trade-offs at my mom's parents' house, where we lived on and off for a while. My younger brother Chris and I eagerly let the heavy metal screen door slam behind us that chilly October day as we raced for a chance at shotgun in our dad Kevin's apple red Toyota Tacoma. For reasons unbeknownst to me, we weren't getting our usual weekend with him, which meant we'd need to cram all of my birthday festivities into an eight-hour window of fun. In the rearview mirror, I saw our mom and stepdad Karl waving us off at the top of the cul-de-sac as we cruised onward toward our next set of grandparents' house.

Billy Ray Cyrus sang *"Achy Breaky Heart"* on the radio as we cruised East on the 10 freeway. Twenty-five minutes and two rights later, we came upon a modest home in Bloomington, California, with a chain-link fence around the property and a choir of wind-chimes harmonizing in the soft breeze. The garage door seemed to stay permanently open at their house, with my grandpa Jim almost surely inside fiddling with his boat and puffing cigars. He was a petite man with a few thin strands of hair combed over the center of his glossy dome, prickly face whiskers, and the grease-stained hands of a mechanic. Loose gravel flew from underneath my heels as I sprinted toward him and called out, *"Grandpa!"* He let out a jolly, *"Hey, girl!"* in his fading Georgia accent and held me tight, like he was unsure when he'd have the chance again.

Inside, I found my grandma Pat slicing up cucumbers and hotdogs to serve for lunch with a generous helping of ranch dressing. She was a larger woman who only wore bright, floral muumuus, with a raspy smoker's voice and an affinity for pirating VHS's. I was her first granddaughter, and she was never shy about telling me how special that was to her.

"Get on over here, girl, and give your grandma a big hug!"

She planted a wet kiss onto my lips, and I could taste the Marlboro Red linger in the air between us as I bolted to the small dining room table. It was decorated with a couple dazzling gift bags and an oversized store-bought cake with the words, *"Happy Birthday, Andi"* piped in pink icing. Next to the cake sat a rectangular envelope addressed to me that I'd come to anticipate every holiday or birthday more than any other gift.

Back then, gift cards had yet to make their debut, and their placeholders were these glossy paper certificates resembling money, with a thick store logo and dollar value displayed on its face. Grandma Pat was famous for gifting us with a whole twenty-five dollars' worth of shiny goodness from Target, and we absolutely loved her for it. She was a sprightly woman with a child-like innocence that contradicted her hoarse tones, who accessorized her tan wool couch with battery operated plush animals. She understood that kids at any age could be in charge of their own present destiny. I knew well before I tore the envelope what was inside that card, and I already had my heart set on the perfect purchase; a Polly Pocket Starlight Castle. On a typical visit, I'd creep down the L-shaped hallway to a small room with wall to wall VHS's labeled in my grandma's tiny scribbled handwriting, sliding my fingertips over each one as I read their title and marveling over her impressive cataloging. Instead, I couldn't wait to hop back in my dad's truck and make our way to Target with my newfound wealth to cash in on Polly's latest pocket surprise.

"Go give your grandparents hugs and kisses and then we'll head out to use that gift certificate, okay?"

Dad ushered Chris and me to the arms of our grandma and grandpa for one last big hug and kiss before leading us through the flimsy plastic screen door, down the step, past the wind chimes, and over the uneven pavement.

"Shotgun!" I demanded as I pushed the passenger seat forward to let Chris squeeze in behind me. My humble, introverted little brother didn't bother to protest. He was used to me beating him to the punch and rarely spoke out against it. I felt like a baby kangaroo in her mother's pouch on the fifteen-minute drive to bullseye paradise bobbing to the motion of my racing pulse and defying gravity with each crack and bump in the road lifting my body from the seat. If children could spontaneously combust from excitement, I would've detonated the moment those double-wide censor doors opened for me, blowing cool, popcorn scented air through my long auburn locks.

I made a beeline for the toy department and shrieked with exhilaration as I shimmied a Polly Pocket Starlight Castle Playset box off of its hook and into my arms, embracing the packaging like a long lost sister. Suspense pulsed through my eager fingertips as I marveled at the heart-shaped, Pepto Bismol pink, castle. Princess Polly and her handsome Prince Caspar were waiting for me inside with their noble steed pulling a carriage fit for a Thumbelina-sized princess. The lake outside of their grand castle was graced with a removable swan. The courtyard and gazebo even lit up. Dad pointed out that with a price tag of only $9.99, I still had cash to spend. This decision would involve careful thought, consideration, research, and time, all of which I had zilch. We had to be returned to mom soon, so he came up with a brilliant solution:

"Why don't we get this now, and then I'll talk to your mom and see if I can pick you up Thursday to take you shopping for the rest. Okay?"

Goodbye always punctured a vein in my heart. As my dad walked us up the steep driveway toward our mom, I mounted his left shoe like a carousel horse and snaked my arms around his shin, tightening my grip with each of his attempts to peel me off gently. Thursday was an eternity away, but my mom gently reminded me that I'd have him all to myself—just daddy and his little girl combing the aisles of Target for the perfect, $15 or less birthday present. Tears licked my cheeks as I watched that red Tacoma fade into the curve of the house-lined road. Thursday. I only had to wait until Thursday.

The climb to Thursday felt like the slow clap scene in *Cool Runnings* when the Jamaican bobsled team's leader Derice convinces the rest of his teammates that they must finish the Winter Olympics race after their gut-wrenching crash. The four men post up on all sides of their sled and carry it over their shoulders to the end, giving one lucky audience member the perfect opportunity to initiate an epic slow clap sequence. I was like Derice carrying my sled to a banner that read "Thursday!," only my sled was actually a paper gift card with a little less than fifteen dollars left on it. Still, as each day passed, the clap grew stronger until finally, it broke out into a roar on TGIF eve. The crowds cheered and the trumpets played. I kissed little babies on their heads and said, *"No, you're the best, Carol!"* at passing strangers who gazed upon the success of my wait. I'd done it. I finally waited five full days, and now it was time to step on the podium and accept my award. My dad and I were going to light up the night in aisle E48, and Target wasn't prepared for the party we were about to ignite.

Instead, the evening fell silent in the dimly lit dining room. My knees pressed against a chair cushion, forming grooved imprints from the pattern, and my arms draped over its back, clutching that $25 Target gift certificate as if it were my entry ticket to the pearly white gates. The peeled back curtains revealed a cul-de-sac full of cars that were in for the night, illuminated by street lights and a hint of the moon trying to fight its way through the thick clouds. *He'll be here. He'll be here. He promised he'd take me, so he'll be here.*

Eventually, I felt my mother's palm on my shoulder. *"Time to go to bed, sweetie. I'm sure he just got caught up."*

As it turned out, aisle E48 would never see Kevin Harrell and his daughter for that party. I had Polly, her pocket, and a little less than fifteen dollars left on a Target gift certificate, but I no longer had my dad. He and his red Toyota Tacoma were suddenly gone, without any note, phone call, or explanation. There was no goodbye. No, "I'm sorry." No, "I love you." He simply didn't exist in my life anymore, overnight. It was as if he slipped out of this world but somehow didn't die. Nobody talked about it. There were no calls to the police, no search parties, and no retracing steps to see if he could be located. As far as I knew, he'd disappeared entirely and yet, nobody seemed to be up in arms about it except for me. One day I was strutting around the playground with my own theme music playing in my head, contemplating what to buy with my remaining birthday funds, and the next, I was a second-grader obsessed with the idea that if her father left right before her birthday, it must have been because she did something wrong. It felt as though Kevin threw a wrench in those conveyer belt child trade-offs, deeming the product as defective and rendering his agreement null and void.

When the dust settled and we all adjusted to life without joint custody, my mom revealed the darkness my dad had been fighting within himself. Alcohol and drugs were the poison in the well, and he'd plummeted all the way to the bottom. This news was meant to release me from the belief that I was to blame, but it hadn't. On the contrary, I wondered what I'd done wrong to make my father turn to these ailments. And so, at the tender age of seven, I began down my own path of darkness as the abandoned little girl, left at baggage claim for someone else to handle.

UNPACKING ABANDONMENT

If I had a dollar for every person I've come across in my life with her own version of abandonment demons to fight off, I'd be writing this book on a yacht right now, sipping Cristal, and eating cocktail shrimp out of an 1897 hand-decorated 24 karat gold platter from Syracuse. I'd have so much cash that I'd blast Benjamins into the ocean out of one of those air cannons and laugh wildly as they floated off into the sea forever. Parental abandonment is unfortunately about as ordinary as catching a common cold, but growing up, I didn't know that. Like most great pains, mine felt unique and unmatched. How could anybody in the world possibly know what it was like to go from being daddy's little girl to an old banana tossed in the trash?

I became obsessed with the idea that I wasn't good enough, pretty enough, smart enough, worthy enough to be loved. I convinced myself that if I could find Kevin, I'd be whole again; I'd be worthy. I'd cry out to him, and he would grovel at my feet and explain to me that it was all some big mistake. That he missed me and thought of me every single day. He became my own personal unicorn hunt, my quest, and my top-secret mission. I wanted to find him because I needed him to tell me that I was loved. His love would fix me. It broke me, and it was the only piece that could glue me back together again.

I always thought my saga started a week before my seventh birthday, staring out that kitchen window in the house at the top of the street, with the curtains peeled back, street lights on, and a cul-de-sac full of cars that were in for the night. Clutching a $25 Target gift certificate and trying not to blink as I waited for the date with my dad that would never come. Maybe I've clung to this story as "the moment" for so long because it felt poetic and finite? In truth, my biological father had abandoned me long before he stopped physically showing up. It wasn't until I began unpacking my issues around abandonment that I became privy to it.

Sometimes it's easier to cling to a slice than to confront the entire pie, and I'd been taking bites out of the same rotten piece for over twenty-three years before I finally noticed there were still seven more slices left untouched. The rest of the pie, the layers I'd yet to dig into, turned out to be even more rancid than the sliver I'd been consuming almost my entire life.

When I started to write this book, I sent a rough draft of this chapter to the most gifted writer I know in real life, my best friend, Alwyn. We frequently bounce our work off one another, and I knew when she chose to wait to talk to me in person that what I'd written was crap. At coffee the following week, she offered her notes along with a question:

"What do you think this chapter is about, Andi?"

Her question took me off-guard. Wasn't it obvious? She'd heard the story a million times in our twelve-year friendship, so she already knew my answer to her question, which posed the real question: What am I missing?

"I know you think this chapter is about your dad leaving, but I think it's actually about how he never protected you even before he left."

Consequently, she was right. I'd been skimming the surface, licking the whipped cream off the top and saving the rest for another day. What I discovered when I began diving into the rest of the pie was that the overall truth remained the same, but my timeline was off entirely. Yes, my biological father abandoned us, but it happened long before he stopped physically showing up. Years before skorts, jelly shoes, and brightly colored snap clips were in style Kevin Harrell had been falling short as a parental figure in my life. All of the good memories I thought I had didn't actually involve anything good; in reality, there was just nothing terrible happening, so my brain logged them into the "not too shabby" folder. Once I became aware of this lost knowledge, everything started to make sense, and the core truth revealed itself: I was never daddy's little girl.

Kevin is a complicated man. I won't pretend to know why he got into drugs and alcohol, but I do know the effects on his children. I was no more than five years old when he first instructed me about what to do if I couldn't wake him up from one of his benders.

"Just shake me and if that doesn't work, pour water over my face."

No problem, dad! I'm your big girl, I've got this!

We had a close call once while my mom was at work. He filled a pot with water and placed it on the stove under high heat before disappearing into his bedroom. I was playing in my room with my Barbie dream house when I smelled something funny and walked out to investigate. Smoke filled the kitchen, and I ran to get the only adult in the house, but Kevin had locked the door and wasn't responding to my pleas. I was four, and all I knew was that there was smoke everywhere, and I needed to protect my brother. I grabbed Chris, locked us both in my room, and started shoving puzzle pieces underneath the door to fill the cracks. I reasoned they'd keep the smoke from coming into the room, which in retrospect, is some damn, clever, out of the box thinking for a kid who couldn't even read yet. My mom walked in the house just in time to get the fire out before any severe damage was done and I was proud of my efforts to hold down the fort until she got home to save the day.

Honestly, all of the real memories I have of him are messed up in one way or another. He was either putting adult responsibilities on my tiny shoulders so he could get his high, or he was punishing me for existing by doing things like pouring hot sauce in my mouth and forcing me to stand in front of a full-length closet mirror and stare at myself until he determined I'd learned my lesson and could spew out the pooling spicy liquid. I stood ears length from him on several occasions where he'd disclaim me if he considered my actions to be unfavorable, passing me off to my mom like a problem he didn't have the energy to solve. He'd always exclaim, *"You really need to get a handle on your daughter"* right in front of me, but I didn't realize the impact it had on me until I began unpacking my story of abandonment.

Looking at the entire pie, it's clear to see why my father left such a profound mark on my own self-love and worth. There was a hole in my heart that was burning with each breath I took. Since I couldn't have his love, I set out on a journey to find it from any and every other male I could. I was looking for whatever I could to fill the gaping void inside of me left by the man who never loved me enough to protect me, forgive me, walk through aisle E48 with me, or stay.

There's an old Irish proverb traced back to R. Taverner that asserts, *"Better the devil you know, than the devil you don't know."*[1] This is the sweet spot: The place where healing occurs. The Devil I didn't know was the one engorging me and eclipsing behind this story of abandonment a week before my seventh birthday. Once I called my relationship with my father by its real name, my heart went through an exorcism. I started projectile vomiting memories and truths that ultimately exposed the demon that had been silently wreaking havoc on my soul. What I'm left with now that I've expelled all the bullshit, is acceptance. Part of this comes with being a parent myself now and knowing that at two, four, six, or any other age, a child isn't to blame for the actions of their parents, nor should kids be treated the way I was. I etched expectations on myself I'd never put on my own children and likewise, expected things from Kevin that I know I'll have to let my kids figure out for themselves. Parents can guide us, but they don't have an overwrite kill switch for our brains they can press if they want us to be someone or something else. I'd never find the answers in my biological father, even if the fairytale happened like I'd envisioned. All in all, he didn't possess the answers, but I did.

Before I started unpacking my bag, this information would've felt like being stuck in an escape room, blind and by myself. Mostly because I wasn't ready to admit I'd been carrying the answer within me all along. It felt more comfortable to link up with the story of daddy's little girl turned abandoned child than admit he was never the father I thought he was. Leaning into this revelation revealed to me that his lack of involvement in my life was really a blessing, not a curse. I was saved from a front-row seat in his unraveling. I didn't have to watch him slowly kill himself. I didn't have to experience police showing up at my home to arrest him on any of the many occasions he landed in jail over the years. Kevin's abandonment shielded me from the trauma that drug and alcohol abuse can lace into a family because I was entirely removed from it all. I was estranged from him. It wasn't a punishment for being an unlovable kid; it was a selfless act amid a series of selfish ones. Once I realized this accidental mercy, I didn't have an excuse not to look inward for the answers.

It hurts when people don't live up to our expectations of them, especially when those people happen to be our parents. We're told that parents are the ones we should be able to depend on for any and everything, but that's simply not always the case. Before a parent becomes a mother or father, one is first, a person. That person sometimes grows with the newfound responsibility of caring for a life beyond his or her own, but having sex and making babies isn't a guarantee that everyone will rise to the occasion of parenting. It takes grit, maturity, and a deep kind of love we can only tap into fully if we love ourselves first. Kevin clearly didn't love himself because he was hiding in the arms of cheap booze and locally cooked meth, so how could I expect him to love me any better?

It's natural to be disappointed and hurt if your parent didn't love you the way you envisioned a parent should love their child. We all have a primitive response to feelings of rejection and abandonment that must be acknowledged. But we must also be willing to look at the entire pie. You can process your affliction while releasing the story you've attached to it. My big exhale was admitting to myself, for myself, that my biological father never really settled into his role as a dad, and that wasn't my fault. I couldn't control him, I couldn't make him show up for me, and I certainly couldn't make him love me. The truth is, I never needed him to in the first place.

The love I was searching for wasn't inside of him. I may have dug out the very first item to make its way into my bag, but I was far from done yet. If I'd been spinning a tale of abandonment ruining my life, what else was I lying to myself about? It was time to discover my truth. So I kept rummaging through the tossed out bag. There was still a lot more work to do and shame was looming on the horizon.

SHAME: NEXT STOP, MASTURBATION STATION

"Shame is a soul eating emotion."

— CARL GUSTAV JUNG

IT WAS A WARM SUMMER EVENING, ONE OF THE LAST I'D SEE before starting high school in a few days, when everything changed. I'm lying in bed when it begins. The itch feels like the first hello from a furniture salesperson.

"Welcome! Can I help you find anything specific today?"

It starts taking shape, but I don't feel the need to acknowledge it yet.

"Oh, I'm just browsing, but thank you."

Still, it hovers like a vulture, circling back and declaring, *"Just so you know, we've got a big special going on right now. Let me know if you need any assistance."*

This tickle is persistent, so I give it a quick nod, reaching my hand down over my pajama pants, and letting my fingertips gently attempt to swipe the discomfort away. That first rub was like a moth to the flame. I've opened up Pandora's box, bit the apple, and pressed the big red button. Like any good salesperson, my itch only grew stronger with each attempt to ditch it.

"Do you like this? It's great for families, and it looks great in any space! Do you need to finance? We have financing! Can I start an order for you?"

I slide my hand underneath my panties to be more precise. *I do like this, but I'm not ready to commit just yet. I'm just browsing, give me some space.* Still, the prickle grows stronger, forcing me to press my index and middle fingers faster and firmer over my right labia. A rush of blood floods my pink lips, warming my entire body like a cup of creamy cappuccino. I'm tingling all the way down to my toes as the tickle builds like a bass drum beat in a rock n' roll song. It shouts, *"But wait, there's more! Let me show you this: It's going to blow your mind!"* and I find myself bewitched by its desire to please me. My body succumbs to the seduction, and I whisper, *"Show me the best you've got"* as the heat rises to my face and escapes through my quickening breath. My hand and the itch work in tandem, and before I know what happened, I find myself the proud new owner of the purchase of a lifetime. There's warm, wet juice garnishing my fingerprints and for a moment while my heart rate begins to stabilize I wonder if I peed myself.

Masturbation. Orgasm. These were dirty foreign words used to describe porn stars and women who chain-smoked and shop-lifted lacy bras from the mall. I was positively clueless about my body and its primal urges because nobody ever discussed sex to me outside of the required school courses where they passed out tampons stapled to tootsie rolls and reinforced the mindset that sex would cause chlamydia, AIDS, and pregnancy. My teacher for seventh-grade sex education was a middle-aged man who wore cargo shorts year-round and looked like he spent his weekends backpacking off a dirt path and collecting unique rocks for his glass-encased collection. Most days, he'd devote a few minutes reading from our textbook and then switch over to an educational video about the penis and vagina, while proceeding to lift a single hairy leg to his chair in the Captain Morgan stance so we could all see his junk through his khaki uniform as he asked if we had any questions. You try paying attention when the outline of a grown man's penis is ten feet from your flushing face for an hour.

So I'm there in my bed, and I just had the most intense experience of my life to date, and I'm now aware of two realities:

1. I'm a sinner.
2. I'm going to do it again.

I'm like Janet in the *Rocky Horror Picture Show*. I've tasted blood, and I want *more, more, more.* Heaven help the wicked because this girl is on fire and she can't escape the flames. My love affair with myself had begun; but every time I'd touch myself, I'd feel a charge of shame flood over me. To the world, I was a sweet, innocent girl, but inside, I was filled with sexual desire that left me feeling vile. You see, I worked up quite a reputation for myself as a "goody-goody, smart girl" over the years.

It started in elementary school when I practically became the local poster child for D.A.R.E. They hooked me in with every cartoon about the dangers of peer pressure, and I was drunk on the alcohol-free Kool-Aid. We all had to write speeches about choosing to be drug free in fifth grade, and mine was chosen for the graduation ceremony. I stood up in front of the entire student body and their parents and pledged my allegiance to a substance-free life in a two-page long story about the man that left me for the bottle and how much better I'd be than he was. Maybe I couldn't have his love, but I'd gain the respect of that audience! They'd praise me for my efforts toward a better America. They'd take pity on me and see my story and know that I was worthy of their love. I was going to earn it. I was going to show them that I could rise above peer pressure and parties and stereotypes. I'd become the perfectly good daughter every father wanted and eventually mine would come to his senses and return once he heard how magnificently accomplished I was.

After my proud display of almightiness in fifth grade D.A.R.E. class, my parents just so happened to gain interest in faith. We began going to church every Sunday and youth group every Wednesday. The church we attended was one of those mega ones that had its own gift shop and cafe, and every week I'd grab a strawberry smoothie and browse the aisles for Bible bookmarks, worship CDs, and "What Would Jesus Do?" bracelets. I'd found a new high to take over the loss of the D.A.R.E. program, and that high was none other than the cross-bearer himself. Oh, I let my Jesus-freak flag soar high and mighty. Arms stretched to the sky, knees on the blue carpet, I had new Kool-Aid to drink, and I was all in: I got baptized. I even persuaded my parents to let me attend a church summer camp that was about five or so days long. There, I got baptized again for the thrill of it. *That's twice in 6 months, for anyone wondering!*

I waltzed into my new middle school that fall with cross necklaces around my neck and conviction on my heart. At the same time, my body started changing and lady puberty was showing up with a vengeance. Although I needed glasses, my parents couldn't afford the ones I wanted, so they teamed up with the optometrist to convince me that ice blue metal frames were cool as shit, and I went for it. I wore chopsticks in my hair, those icicles on my freckled face, and the extra fifteen pounds that came with having my genetic makeup, or maybe also eating nothing but Lays B.B.Q. Chips with chocolate pudding every day. I wrote "I love Jesus" all over my folders and I was in the show choir, which wasn't a sign of coolness back in my day, despite winning championships. We didn't have shows like *Glee* to glorify us, and there were approximately zero cheerleaders or football players in our group. Our choreographer was a tiny petite blonde woman who couldn't stand me and would always make me a "box girl" which meant I was stuck doing half-assed versions of all the dance numbers on a literal box because she didn't want the fat kids taking up space on the floor. What I'm trying to tell you here is boys didn't like me. There wasn't a single quirk about me that jumped out to a guy and screamed, "datable!" However, several things gave off the "Jesus is my boyfriend" vibe and well, who wants to compete with that? Okay, fine. Nobody was lining up to duke it out with J.C. anyway, but you know, I certainly wasn't making it easy on anyone if they'd wanted to do so.

But in the summer of 2000 when I was getting ready to tackle my first year of high school, something dramatic happened. My mom realized her at home hair dying services (highlight cap included) were going to give us both P.T.S.D. and started taking us to an actual salon for our hair. *Goodbye, skunk streaks!* I got contacts and then proceeded to throw them in the trash because they were bulky and annoying. But then, I went and got new frames that didn't make me look like an 85-year-old librarian. My grandma passed her old rusty stationary bike down to me, and I got super into a Paula Abdul workout video my mom had purchased and left for dead in the TV console. I scaled back on the B.B.Q. Chip and pudding cup combo and started reaching for apples on purpose. Suddenly, in a summer's time, your girl was looking cute!

I waltzed into high school like Laney Boggs in *She's All That*, post-makeover. Okay, maybe I was more like Drew Barrymore in *Never Been Kissed*, but you catch my drift. Suddenly boys were paying attention to me, passing me notes, and even leaving me presents in my locker. One tall, skinny boy in my English class asked me to coffee, and I genuinely laughed in his face because I thought he was joking. It was the beginning of a new era for me, one where I was suddenly a young woman of interest. I'd spend the next fifteen years battling disordered eating and body dysmorphia, but that's a story for later.

The big guy upstairs and I were still best friends, but I was less outward about it. I stopped decorating my neck with crosses as if I was warding off evil spirits in first period English and replaced all of my W.W.J.D. folder paraphernalia with photos of my friends, favorite bands, and inspirational quotes. Halfway into my freshman year, I started taking a drama class, and there, I found my people.

Word quickly spread about the adorable little freshman with dimples and freckles who was outgoing and funny, with the innocence of a virgin. People in the theatre were enthralled with me and me with them. I'd never been around people who were so open, honest, and free. They were unapologetic. They kissed boys, kissed girls, kissed whoever they damn well pleased. They undressed in front of one another, sat on each other's laps, and told jokes that were erotic, controversial, and crude. Never had I ever seen anything like it in all of my life, and I was hooked.

ANDI FRANKLIN

Likewise, most of them had never seen the likes of me inside the fourth wall. They were enamored with my childlike purity. I was a living organism inside of a petri dish. An oddity they couldn't quite wrap their heads around. Surprise erupted in the room as they watched me work a dramatic scene. They couldn't believe I had so much depth. It seemed impossible and charming to them that I'd never even experienced a kiss and could still somehow keep up with them and their humor, their wit, their raciness.

I melted into them like butter on a warm dinner roll. They stretched my horizons like a vibrant sunset. That theatre became my home and the people, my people. They continued to be provocative, and I continued to be innocent, and we all lived together in beautiful acting harmony. Only, when we got off the stage, their scenes ended, but mine never did. I was cloaked under the blanket of innocence. It had become such a massive part of my identity within this new home of mine that I was sure if I unveiled myself, I'd destroy the very fabric of our tender relationship.

One night, sophomore year, we were having a cast party. One of the older girls said we could all use her aunt's house for the party because nobody would be home. So we laughed, ate chips, and a few people drank in secret. Then we all cozied up in our sleeping bags in the living room. Somebody suggested we play ten fingers. I'd never played, and there was a roar of laughter and excitement over the idea that everyone present got to take my ten fingers' virginity. A beautiful older girl with thick stark black, wiry hair explained the rules to me and began with her first confession:

"Never have I ever had sex in a car."

Everyone began howling as two people put a finger down. Mine were obviously all still intact.

46

Next person.

"Never have I ever made out with a girl."

All of my fingers remained tall and proud.

"Never have I ever hooked up with Steve in the green room!"

Direct attempts to destroy select people in this game were highly encouraged. Then, somebody went in for the kill.

"Never have I ever masturbated!"

My heart started to race, and I anxiously looked around the room as every single finger dropped but mine.

"Omg, I was just kidding! I wanted to see if there was anyone who wouldn't put his or her finger down. Andi, you've never masturbated?!"

Suddenly, I was on the stage. All eyes were glued to me. I could hear faint laughter in the distance, but it was hard to hear over my quickening breath. My thumping heartbeat. My racy lie. Someone pressed on in disbelief.

"No way! Are you serious? You've never tried it? It's amazing, you need to try!"
"Guys, come on. It's Andi! She's sweet and innocent, so of course, she hasn't!"
"Omg, you're so adorable. I just want to eat you up!"

I wanted to tell them, really, I did. But being the innocent one seemed to be the only role I could fill well, and I wasn't willing to risk losing that. So, I let them laugh and gawk at me like a circus animal because I was too embarrassed, nervous, and ashamed to admit to a room full of people that I was just like them. After all, What Would Jesus Do if He got wind of my new hobby? Probably nail himself to a cross all over again and declare, *"That's it! That's the last straw! I'm done with these sinful humans!"* So I got to keep being the wee little lamb to my friends and the filthy dirty night caresser to myself. Best of both worlds? Hardly. My definition of wrong needed a good ole' fashioned chimney sweep, but unfortunately, Bert was too preoccupied with Mary Poppins to help. Now that I'm thinking about it, Dick Van Dyke looked pretty damn good dancing around with all that soot on his face, all sweaty and sexy and, excuse me one moment, I'll be right back.

UNPACKING SHAME

Friends, isn't it mind-blowing the kind of pressure we put on ourselves to fit into a mold of what or who we think we're supposed to be? I mean, what in God's green earth do we think we're doing by denying the straight-up gift we were given to feel and experience pleasure? It's like when we go to a birthday party and skip the cake because we're trying to be good. Look, Becky, there's nothing noble about skipping the birthday cake. It's delicious and enjoyable, and somebody baked that cake with the intention of you enjoying it. Eat the damn cake!

We're also created as women to feel pleasure, not just men. Not just women that look like Angelina Jolie. Not just that one woman you always see in the pickup line at your kids' school who looks so put together and perfect and you're sure she farts rainbows and never forgets to shower. Orgasms aren't solely reserved for the Adonises and Aphrodites of this world. They belong to you, and me, and the person sitting across from you right now as you read this book (but don't look or you'll never be able to see this person again without thinking of their "O" face!).

Had I realized this in high school, I'm 99% positive I would've saved myself from years of pain, abuse, and painfully awkward relationships and situations. But alas, I was slow to learn and quick to pretend I knew everything. And so, the goody-goody lived on in secret. All hail the queen of innocence as she sits on her throne of lies with her hand down her panties. The fact was, I didn't just touch myself, but I loved touching myself. Every second building up to an orgasm felt like the climb to 13,000 feet in a small aircraft right before jumping out and freefalling in the sky. But the minute I released, it was as if my parachute jammed and I was plummeting headfirst to my demise. How could something so liberating also seize all the air from my lungs and leave me paralyzed in fear? I needed to uncover the answer because it was keeping me from embracing my sexuality even now, as a happily married woman in her thirties.

In her 2010 TEDx talk titled "The Power of Vulnerability," Dr. Brené Brown refers to shame as *"the most powerful, master emotion"* adding, *"It is the fear that we're not good enough."* [1] Listening to her words lit a candle in my brain, which is what I envision "lightbulb" moments looked like before Benjamin Franklin discovered electricity. There was a name for the lump in my throat that crept up every time I pleasured myself; she was none other than shame herself. Shame, as it turns out, was the consequence of my life as an overachieving do-gooder. The church taught me to fear God, to fear sex, and most of all, to fear myself and my desires. It groomed me to err on the side of caution in regards to things I didn't know much about, and I knew absolutely nothing about the primal urges I was having. As a result, when I gave into them, it felt like I was disrupting the natural order of the universe, betraying my parents, and condemning myself to eternal damnation. When you spend your entire adolescence in the shadows of what and who you believe you're supposed to be to have any value or worth, it's a cluster fuck to dismantle.

Meeting the love of my life wasn't a garlic necklace warding off my shame vampire, or a loophole in the contract or a pass go, collect $200 type of deal. My shame was more active than a FitBit on a marathon runner's wrist, running rampant on my self-esteem and silently Charlie-horsing not only my sex life but my humanness. The discussion of female pleasure is more taboo than admitting you own a Nickelback album, which is why so many of us grow up believing all things sex-related are either to make men happy or make a baby. We affiliate masturbation with men and even shove them into a box based on how openly they talk about it, how often they do it, and whether or not they use outside stimulation for their process. Teenage boys are expected to watch a lot of porn and keep a bottle of lotion on their night-stand, but if an adult man does the same thing, we assume he's some creep who lives in his parent's basement and has a foot fetish. Likewise, if a young girl or woman does any of the above, she's immediately labeled gross, slutty, loose, dirty, and out of her damn mind like a woman on day seven of a juice cleanse.

Sometimes I think men look at a woman's sexuality like it's the final level of a video game and once they win, they'll unlock all the secrets of the universe to the poor defenseless female, bestowing magical powers upon her that enable her to perform like Jenna Jameson in the bedroom and Martha Stewart in the kitchen. He, of course, will bless her with his legendary dick and switch to a multiplayer mode so that she, too, can level up and achieve orgasm. Only, she's been a damsel for so long that she doesn't want to risk losing this new life, so she fakes orgasms and keeps his house clean just to keep him happy. She never experiences real pleasure herself, but the sex is okay I guess, and she gets to have kids and watch *The Bachelor* every week so, who can complain?

As bad as men are about women's sexual satisfaction, our female peers can be even worse. Nobody invites the candid-about-sex girlfriend to hot yoga class because *"She's tasteless."* Never mind that she has been in a monogamous relationship for ten years, that girl is trash because women don't talk about those sorts of topics. In my experience, when you talk about sex, orgasms, etc. in front of other women, especially in the mommy world, they look at you like you're exotic but not the good kind of exotic, like a tropical bird. They deem you as more like a Zika carrying mosquito that needs to be swatted down and destroyed before it spreads anymore of its disease to others. *She says she experiences frequent orgasms and believes all women should have access to this sorcery? WITCH! She's a witch!*

I think a lot of it has to do with the fact that many women are in hiding. The amount of ladies I've spoken with who've never experienced an orgasm is staggering and downright criminal. The common denominators I've unearthed from these women are that they fake it and never touch themselves. Ladies, we have to stop faking orgasms. You don't have to talk to a single person about masturbation, and you certainly don't have to write about it publicly in a book like I am. However, if the concept of touching yourself brings up big feelings of shame and discomfort,

I want to encourage you to dig deeper and figure out why. Why does the idea of tapping into this gift of pleasure frighten you?

To be clear, I'm not saying you should open a PornHub account or have permanently pruned fingertips from excessive contact with bodily fluids or run away to a European sex show or anything quite as wild as that. Instead, I want to encourage you to get in sync with your body. What I realized once I called shame by its name, was that touching myself was actually a wonderfully natural thing and it also taught me what I like and don't like, which I was then able to bring to the bedroom with my husband later in life. We all need to learn about our bodies and explore them to find out what turns us on and to discover what works for us. When you take the time to get to know yourself, your romantic relationships are better and you can offer your spouse more because you're able to show them how to please you, as opposed to pretending to orgasm and finding reasons not to engage in anything sexual.

Unpacking the shame I carried over masturbation was tricky. Trying to convince my brain I wasn't a good girl gone bad, flying off the handle, took time. It took grace. I had to admit my fandom for pleasure before I could embrace the beauty of learning about my body. I had to get a little uncomfortable and do things I'd never done like look at my vagina in a mirror, so I could understand what areas were pleasure sources and which were for functionality. Have you heard about those women who don't know that you pee and bleed from two different holes? Maybe you're one, and I'm not throwing shade your way because I was one of those people, too. I was so out of touch with my own body that I didn't even know there was a difference between the urethral and vaginal opening. I'll never forget seeing a video pop up on Facebook about it and legitimately gasping out loud in shock.

You're telling me there have been two holes this entire time?!

The truth is, everyone will tell you that you're responsible for yourself. Your happiness. Your health. Your success. They'll reiterate how you're responsible for all parts of yourself, except your pleasure. No, apparently pleasure is the only part of you that you're not accountable for; and if you do take the lead, there's a thick shame cloud cast overhead. So instead, we place it entirely on the shoulders of another human being for the rest of eternity. We make it his or her responsibility to *"make us orgasm"*—Like it's as simple as pressing a button on our backs. This implies our partner is somehow in control of our bodies, instead of us. Meaning, we don't live as autonomously as we'd like to believe.

We want to believe our pleasure lies in someone else's hands because we have so much shame and misunderstanding wrapped around it. But the truth is simple: Your pleasure is your responsibility. It's more than right spot, right time. Your partner can do everything right and you can be so in your head that it doesn't matter. That's because they aren't in charge of your pleasure, you are. And it goes so much further than in the bedroom. You've got to turn yourself on, and you've got to charge up your life.

Pleasure exists in all areas of life, not just sex. Finding pleasure in the company you keep, in the books you read, in the food you eat. Finding pleasure in nature, in sunshine, in a cool breeze on your skin. Finding pleasure in yourself. Learning to delight in who you are and how you think. Studying your edges so that when you see them move in bed you aren't startled by their presence—feeling love for your body exactly where it is. You're accountable for your pleasure and when you realize that, sex becomes more about connection and less about exchange. It takes away performance pressure and allows both partners to be open about their likes, dislikes, limits, fantasies, and so forth.

Let me paint this picture a little more vibrantly: Have you ever bought a piece of furniture from Ikea? They come unassembled, and all of the directions are written in Swedish, which is great if you can read Swedish, but not so pleasant for the rest of us. The language barrier forces you to rely on pictures and sheer willpower to get your bookshelf, desk, or bed frame built. Each project feels like trying to solve the formula for time travel and usually several hours and curse words later you end up with a sturdy enough looking piece of furniture and a couple extra bolts and screws. The extras are baffling, but you're unwilling to take it apart and start that hell all over again, so you tuck them away and pretend they never existed, hoping for the best and eventually forgetting it was never adequately built, from the get go. Sure, it can hold up for a while, but eventually it comes crashing down after you tossed your keys on it like a cherry blanketed in a whipped cream avalanche. Both the cherry and the keys were trying to make their home on top of a precarious structure. Eventually, they were always going to plummet without a solid foundation to support them.

The same applies when we treat certain parts of ourselves like extras we can toss in a drawer and forget all about. Our bodies aren't poorly made Ikea furniture. Every nook and cranny of us was by design and meant to be utilized. When we exclude parts of our blueprint, we can't live up to the potential we were created to obtain. We cheapen our own product when we refuse to go back and find out where the missing bolts and screws belong. If we truly see our bodies as temples, then we should feel honored to have the opportunity to live within their walls and experience all of their glorious gifts. We should treat them with tender care and know all of their edges. We should build our cells and our souls up using every last available tool given to us because we weren't created to leave the most fulfilling parts of ourselves dormant. We weren't created to leave *any* parts of ourselves dormant.

Consequently, shame tries to convince us we don't need every piece. It says we're good enough without "that bit there and this bit here." It makes us fear tearing down the structure that appears to have kept us safe all these years to reassemble ourselves using every last bolt and screw we've been given. But a foundation without all the pieces cannot hold forever. It's a lie. An illusion of safety, all the while, filling up and getting more unstable by the minute. It creates stress on parts of us that should have an even weight distribution, were they crafted correctly. It's why we find ourselves restless, moody, self-conscious, envious, stressed, overwhelmed, and so on. Think about it.

Imagine a tea pot unable to release steam. As the water heats up, pressure builds in the pot's belly—pressure that's meant to be released. But if the steam has nowhere to go, it'll cause the pot to explode. You and I are the teapots and our bodies are the water. Orgasms release oxytocin; they reduce stress, and they create a closer bond between partners. They're the steam we expel to keep the pot from exploding. We've got no problem tending to swollen, tired muscles, applying creams, foam rolling, getting massages to work them out. So why don't we treat our sex organs with the same care? Why do we shy away from this vital relief our bodies yearn for naturally?

I want you to know, in case nobody has ever said it to you, that orgasm isn't a dirty word and enjoying the deep connection and pleasure you get from intimacy is nothing to be ashamed of savoring. Shame and embarrassment have no place within us. They're what keep us from knowing the difference between our urethra and vagina. They deprive us from experiencing the most beautiful natural parts of our humanity. If you're feeling wobbly, then it's time to start the undoing so you can rebuild with all of your pieces. You, me, and the dolphins were born to experience the rush and liberation of our sexuality. It's a gift we were born with, not a curse. Not a punishment. Not a test. Not an impurity. It's truly a beautiful, bonding inheritance.

TRAUMA: THE BOY WITH
THE CROOKED SMILE

*"Anything that's human is mentionable, and anything that is
mentionable can be more manageable. When we can talk about
our feelings, they become less overwhelming, less upsetting, and
less scary. The people we trust with that important talk can
help us know that we are not alone."*

– FRED ROGERS

KYLE TOLD ME HE WAS THINKING ABOUT KILLING HIMSELF.

Our drama teacher, Mr. Stevens, wiggled the play he wrote
himself into the spring schedule and forced the entire class to
participate, which meant we had two full casts. It was an exas-
perating tale of young children living in a mental institution, and
I desperately wanted the role of Charlie, the dark and cynical
pyro. But of course, I got typecast as Sarah, the shy and timid
little girl who created an imaginary friend to help her cope with
her abusive father. Kyle and I had to work a few scenes together,
and that's when he began confiding in me that he wanted to die.
Insert my sensational savior syndrome here: I was convinced all

he needed was a good friend to guide him back to the light, and I fervently committed myself to the task.

Kyle saw my efforts as divine intervention and concluded all signs were pointing toward a once-in-a-lifetime romance opportunity between the two of us. Personally, I didn't have any interest in him other than to fulfill my bloodlust for saving people, but he was unconventionally charming and persistent. He began writing me love letters with impressive hand-drawn artwork of the two of us bowling, sitting in a movie theatre, or laughing over a pizza dinner, which was both flattering and perplexing. I continued to politely decline his advances; conversely as a last-ditch effort, he illustrated a scenario where I missed out on true love because I was too afraid and essentially dared me to take a chance on him. At that time in my life, I was infamous among my inner circle for never refusing a dare, no matter how wild, so I took the bait and agreed to give him a shot to prove me wrong. After all, what was the worst that could happen?

Kyle towered over my 5'4 frame at just under six feet tall, with broad shoulders hovering over his recently trimmed build and a crooked smile that always reminded me of the Joker. He was charismatic and sarcastic, with a thunderous laugh. When he'd get upset, his sharp face turned ruby red with passion. Kyle had an endearing way about him, the sort of roguish charm that only narcissists possess, but of course, I hadn't put my finger on what to call it at the time. Instead, I found myself intrigued by his teenage angst and immersed in solving the riddle that was him. His allure was matched by his intellect, and we spent countless hours on the phone discussing everything from life's greatest mysteries to the undeniable talent of the Red Hot Chili Peppers. I found him attractive in an unconventional yet captivating way and had grown fond of him as a friend, so I couldn't understand why I was struggling to let him in as anything more. It was as if my head was willing, but my body was activating its fight or flight response any time he tried to lean into me for affection. I tried to stop our relationship before it started on the phone the same evening he forced his lips to mine for the first time, but Kyle already had me pegged.

"I like you, and you like me. You're just afraid that I'm going to hurt you like your dad did. But I won't. Stop blaming me for your dad's crimes and let me in."

Kyle loved to tell me what I felt about things. He was an expert at inserting his own opinions into my mouth and claiming they were mine all along. Every word that slithered off his tongue was methodical and calculated, meant to propel himself forward toward his goals, and in this instance, I was the target of his venomous bite. I allowed him to talk me in and out of whatever he wanted. *Yes, we should be together. No, I guess I don't need to see those friends anymore. Yes, let's spend all of our free time at your house. No, you're right. I shouldn't go to that event or listen to that song anymore that so-and-so dedicated to me in the first grade.*

He was the lighter fluid, and I was the match, burning the bridges to anyone who didn't understand how a girl like me could be with a guy like him. Friends who declared him an asshole (of which, there were many) faced the chopping block and found themselves trimmed from my life like fat on a T-bone steak. Kyle constantly reminded me that anyone who wasn't for us, was against us and clearly jealous of our high school love, and I believed him. Over the summer, I was hired for my first professional performing job as one of three female leads in a show called "G.I. Jills" at the Corona Civic Light Opera

House, which only further isolated me from my friendships. A rigorous rehearsal schedule and two-week show run meant my free time was limited, and what little I had to give was reserved for Kyle without question. By the time we walked into our senior year of high school, I only had a handful of companions left to my name—the faithful few who were happy for me, or at least, pretended to be.

By then, I was completely brainwashed. Lines began to blur, and my moral compass was no longer listening to the tiny figures on my shoulder; instead, I was taking direct orders from Kyle. It started innocently enough. We'd make out, and occasionally he'd try and shove his hand down my pants, though, he was usually unsuccessful because I wore skin-tight jeans. I assumed this was just how teenage boys and high school relationships went, but one night, I asked my mom to listen in on a phone conversation I was having with him because I needed to know if it was me, or if something was wrong here. Kyle was on the other line expressing his sexual frustration with me and how he needed me to give more than I was. When we hung up, my mom encouraged me to give a little more. All she knew, of course, was that I grew up an extremely sheltered little girl and had an affinity for being a do-gooder. She was just trying to help me live a bit more on edge. She didn't want me having sex or anything like that, but you know, everything else was left on the table. Honestly, this memory haunts my mom, but it makes me proud of her. I lived my entire life up until that moment, feeling ashamed of my sexuality, and there she was, telling me it was okay to be a sexual creature. Unfortunately, it was the wrong guy for cheerleading, but she never could've known that.

That fall, the intensity of the relationship progressed. After school, he'd bring me to his house while his parents worked and lead me to his bed, where he'd practically rip off my pants. The entire charade made me extremely uncomfortable. I'd protest and try to pull his face up from my crotch, but he was so much stronger and would pin my arms to the bed. I learned quickly that faking an orgasm was my only way out of this situation, so that's what I did. Protest. Get pinned. Fake orgasm. Give a blow job. Happy guy, happy lie. I never got used to it, but what did I know? I was a reformed Jesus freak on the brink of what should've been a sexual awakening. Clearly, I just needed to be broken in, and Kyle was undoubtedly dedicated to breaking me. Occasionally I'd find an excuse not to come over until his stepmom got home, so he couldn't pounce on me, but most of the time I just did what he wanted. I was a rag doll in the jaw of a grizzly bear, a play toy for him to do whatever he pleased with me.

Sometime after Thanksgiving our senior year, on a crisp autumn afternoon, Kyle hinted he had a surprise as we drove to his house after school got out. He told me to get naked and lay in his bed, belly down. I didn't know what to make of the request, but I trusted him for some reason, so I did as he asked. Next thing I knew, he was entering me, anally, and my entire body tightened in pain and panic. I honestly cannot remember if he finished or not. I don't know how long it lasted. It was as if I left my body. All I remember is him climbing off of me and walking to the bathroom without saying a word. I heard the shower turn on, and a few moments later, he told me to join him and wash off. I could hardly lift my body from the bed, but I did. I was terrified of what would happen to me if I didn't. But in the shower, he was tender. He led his fingertips lightly across my body and held me close as if we'd just shared something sacred and holy. As the warm water washed the filth off my body, I began wondering if I simply hadn't made myself clear enough for him. *Should I have said those "nos" louder? Maybe he didn't hear me. Maybe it was my fault? He'd never intentionally hurt me. This is all one big misunderstanding.* Even if deep down, I knew the truth because I'd seen the aggression before when he held me down and forced his mouth on my vagina. Even if I had muscle pains from trying to push him off of me. Even if he'd forced me into our first date, first kiss, and now apparently, my first experience with sexual intercourse. He loved me, and this is just what high school boys did, right?

A few weeks later, Kyle had a cold, and I was headed to his house with a care package like a good little Red Riding Hood. The guy could barely speak or stand, but wouldn't you know it? He wanted to go down on me and me on him. This time I capitalized on the advantage of not being sick, and was able to overpower him.

"You're sick, no! And I have to leave for Shelly's house anyway. Get some rest, I'll call you later. I love you."

Too sick to really fight it, he let me leave and off to Shelly's I hurried. We cozied in her bed, babysitters' club style, and girl talked about school, friends, and boys. I giggled and exclaimed, *"Kyle is so crazy! I just dropped off a care package for him because he's sick and he was trying to force himself down on me."*
Shelly's smile slid off her face.

"Did you tell him not to?"

"Well yeah, but you know how guys are. He didn't this time because he was too sick, but usually, he'll just hold me down."

She grabbed both my hands and looked me square in the eyes to emphasize her next words.

"Andi, that's not normal, and it isn't okay. That's sexual harassment. You need to tell your mom!"

If you've never been in an abusive relationship, then I understand how this sounds from the outside looking in, but I genuinely couldn't fully see what was right in front of my face until someone I loved and trusted pointed it out. Yet, the moment she spoke, I broke down in tears because I knew she was right. I didn't even tell her about the rape because, at that point, I still hadn't processed it. All I knew as I lifted my body from her bed and practically ran out of her house to go home and collapse into my mother, was that Kyle's smokescreen was gone, and I finally caught a glimpse of the monster he really was.

I called and broke up with him that night. I knew if I approached him with the truth, he'd find a way to convince me I was crazy or overreacting and I also knew I could never be alone with him again, so I lied. I used the oldest trick in the Christian handbook and blamed it on the big guy himself. *I just feel God calling us to break up, I'm sorry. It's not you, it's not me, it's God.* I mean, who could argue with that? If I left the story here, you'd probably think it was traumatic enough, but unfortunately, this isn't where the tale ends. Rape, as it turns out, was only the intermission. Kyle had a way to go with his performance, and I was his involuntary costar.

My mom put me in therapy almost immediately. It wasn't until I was a few sessions in, when I knew I could trust my new therapist, Grace, that I confided about the afternoon where he took it to the next level. Her eyes met mine softly with concern as I detailed what happened, adding it to the list of harassment we were discussing. Yet again, I found myself utterly unaware of the gravity of my abuse until it was articulated out loud to me.

"Andi, that's rape. He raped you, honey."

Rape? Did she just say rape? It didn't seem possible that a word so foul could apply to my life. Why didn't I piece it together? What was wrong with me that a man raped me, and my reaction was to wonder if I was the problem? With my permission, she spoke separately to my mom about this new information, and my parents wanted to go straight to the police. But I wouldn't let them, and honestly, my therapist agreed with me. The idea of spending my senior year in a courtroom recapping the vivid details of my trauma sounded worse than death and Grace cautioned my parents that most rapists walk free because it's too difficult to prove in a court of law. So back to high school, I sheepishly crawled. I saw my rapist every day in drama class and tried to avoid his attempts to pass notes my way or corner me into a discussion. Then, I made an error in judgment that almost kept me from graduating. I told my best friend at the time that I'd been raped, and she spilled the tea to everyone else, including Kyle.

This is high school, dear friends. High school concocts a world within a world where people who aren't exactly children but aren't quite adults yet spend six-plus hours a day together and get minor choices throughout like, what elective to choose or where to go off campus for lunch. High schoolers are like the paparazzi of education: Everybody walks around waiting for shit to hit the fan, any shit at all, in hopes they can be the ones to break the story first and claim glory as the person with the juiciest slice of post-pubescent pie. I naively expected my friend to go against the status quo and carry my secret, but she didn't. And that's when life began to unravel at the seams.

The saga of Andi and Kyle split sixth-period advanced drama into two parts: the people who believed me, and the people who didn't. I neither confirmed nor denied the rumors, but they formed their opinions none the less, and some people I thought were my friends started calling me a liar and a slut behind my back, often within ear range. Kyle didn't take the exposure well, either. I don't ever recall him actually denying the claims, at least not to me, but he was surely going to make me foot the bill for it and pay for it, I did.

You see, I'd grossly underestimated him. I assumed if I just kept my head down, he would leave me alone, but that isn't how a narcissist works. Kyle began verbally harassing me at school as if it were his senior thesis project. He was in charge of the morning announcements and did a dedication to "his ex-girl-friend who shattered his heart" on Valentine's Day, playing "our song" across the speakers for the entire school to hear. He yelled accusations like, "You're a miserable bitch!" across the quads at me while I made my way to the third period. There was even an altercation in the theatre one day where his sharp face turned ruby red with the passion of a thousand suns as he shouted obscenities and charged toward me with such a fury that fellow classmates had to form a protective barrier around me using their bodies as shields. I looked like a V.I.P. being ushered from a hostile situation by the secret service as my friends pushed their way through Kyle and led me to grab my belongings, so I could get the hell out of dodge.

School had become unbearable, and my last resort was to make an appointment with the Vice Principal in hopes that he could help in some way, any possible way. I tapped my toes nervously in a metal-framed chair as I waited for the secretary to call my name. News may have spread faster than a California wildfire among my peers, but I hadn't actually spoken about what was going on with anyone other than a few select women, and now I was going to not only talk to a man about it for the first time, but a man I'd no prior rapport with my entire high school career. Mr. LeDuke opened his door and offered me a seat inside. My voice cracked as I explained briefly what was happening to me under his roof.

"My ex-boyfriend raped me, and now he's harassing me at school. He yells at me in the halls and even got in my face screaming in drama last week. I cry all the time, I'm afraid to be here, and I don't know what to do."

LeDuke wasn't impressed. He clasped his hands behind his neck, forming wings with his elbows, and leaned back in his chair.

"I know how you drama kids like to over-exaggerate sometimes, Andi. I think the best thing you can do for yourself here is just let it go."

Then, (and I shit you not, this really happened) he lunged his body forward, threw his hands on the desk with the enthusiasm of someone who just realized the cure for cancer or something, and started to sing to the tune of the Beatles hit, "Let it Be."

"Let it go, let it go, let it go, let it go! Whisper words of wisdom, let it go!"

My lungs collapsed. I felt crushed under the weight of his janky, out-of-tune rendition of advice. There I was, doing exactly what they say you should do if you're being bullied or harassed at school; and instead of protection or comfort or even just some belief in what I was brave enough to share, the Vice Principal offered me an explanation for what he considered a distorted perception of what was really going on, and serenaded me with a remix to go with it.

That was the day I stopped attending most of my classes. High school, as I came to know it, wasn't a safe place for me to be any longer. While other students were applying for colleges and making the most of senior year, I was showing up just long enough to be counted as in attendance for the day so that my parents wouldn't get a phone call, before heading to Jamba Juice and Ikea to walk around and be as far away from Kyle and his assassination games as possible. If my school wasn't going to keep me safe, I'd have to do it myself, so I did. In fact, the only reason I graduated high school at all is that most of my teachers liked me so much as a student before my life fell apart, that they allowed me to turn in homework and take makeup tests outside of class. As for the less flexible teachers, I was able to take night school for their classes to catch up and graduate with the rest of my peers.

I was supposed to make my big directorial debut that spring with Charlie Brown, the first musical my high school would ever take on thanks to my detailed proposal the year prior. I was meant to perform a powerful dramatic piece in the Fullerton theatre festival that would launch my acting career, take over Disneyland with my friends for grad night, and leave tear stains on yearbooks as I penned beautiful dedications about how great our final year together was and how much I'd miss everyone, but I didn't achieve any of those dreams. Everything went on without me, of course. The curtains were called, Disneyland was littered with gleeful teenagers from my hometown, and yearbooks were filled with sweet words and phone numbers. As for me, all I wanted to do was get the hell out of there. I wanted to be as far away from Kyle, Mr. Stevens, Mr. LeDuke, and everyone who was slamming me behind my back and to my face, as possible.

By the time Kyle was done with me, I felt like I had died. My innocence had been stolen. I was still technically a virgin by societal standards, which friends would so callously remind me if I dared to bring up what occurred.

"I mean, at least it was just anal. It's not like he took your virginity or got you pregnant or anything like that."

And so, I learned to either laugh about it, speak robotically like a historian reporting on something that transpired thousands of years ago, or pretended it never happened. I shoved the pain and fear and utter disgust with myself and my body deep down in mental limbo where they couldn't hurt me or give others the power to destroy me with their opinions. I developed a thick coat of cement over my heart to protect myself, so I'd never have to experience another Kyle as long as I lived.

UNPACKING TRAUMA

Looking back, there were so many red flags that I'm shocked I couldn't see the giant neon "do not date this manipulative creep" sign hovering over his head. I was so desperate to fill the gaping hole inside my heart I believed my biological father left, that I stopped running credit checks and gave anyone a key who was persistent enough to try. Plus, abusers tend to be the most persistent of them all. There's a reason criminals choose dingy motels to commit their crimes. They're usually worn down and trashed, so the owner is willing to give a key to anyone as long as he or she can pay. There are typically no room checks, no house cleaning routines to interrupt the deadly deeds. There's mainly just some cash, and a key, and an extended stay of privacy for the psycho to carry out his or her diabolical plans. I was the motel, and Kyle reigned as my tenant. He paid me in compliments, and his confident, authoritative tone suggested that I don't mess with his reasoning, so I didn't. I just took the cash, handed over the key, and let him claim space. At the tender age of seventeen, I believed this was the love I deserved. I thought Kyle was as good as it was going to get for a baggage ridden girl like me.

Perhaps the craziest part about the entire experience was that initially after calling things off with him, even though I was now consciously aware of the abuse, I still missed him. There was this distorted part of me that felt bad for hurting his feelings and "breaking his heart." Kyle had unlocked a new level of psychological bullying I'd never witnessed before, and I really felt guilty for not only his emotions but also for inconveniencing our friends in the process. Saying that out loud is hard because it forces me to admit how easy it was for him to control me. All my life, I was told that I was above average. I was talented, bright, unique, and wise. How could I possess all of these alleged gifts and not see this horror coming? How did I let him sink his razor-sharp teeth into me like a great white shark?

I adopted a favorite quote during this time in my life, credited to "anonymous" that says, *"A man who knows everything, knows he knows nothing."* It was my senior quote underneath the photo of me in the yearbook, but I didn't understand how it applied to that specific stage until I began digging into this within the last year. My problem was rooted in a belief that I knew everything. My confidence in my wisdom is what pushed me to sit with Kyle in the first place. I thought I was a teenage prophet able to solve the world's problems, whether it involved finding the perfect eyeshadow shade to match a friend's outfit, interpreting the Bible, or helping a classmate work through his suicidal thoughts. I believed I was a hotshot, the Wikipedia of adolescent affairs; your go-to-girl in time of questioning or need, but I was just a kid, like everyone else. I'd barely any life experience, so when trauma hit me, my toolbox was filled with cobwebs and an I.O.U.

And when I did finally step outside of myself and try to reach for help, I was denied. My therapist told me reporting wouldn't yield any results, my teacher didn't step in when Kyle's spit was spraying my face, and my Vice Principal told me to let it go as my ex-boyfriend, and assaulter, continued to harass me whenever I was brave enough to show up to school. Being sodomized was traumatizing, but being unprotected by adults afterward was arguably worse. It taught me men weren't a safe haven for me. They were unreliable, cruel, and pretentious. This lack of faith in men only fueled me to work even harder to be talented, bright, unique, and wise. I felt I needed an upper hand at all times. I didn't want a partner, I wanted someone I could puppeteer so I could always keep them close enough to stay but never quite close enough to hurt me. Of course, it didn't really work. As you continue progressing through this book, you'll find plenty of others I let my guard down around, all in a feeble attempt to love and be loved. Still, I subconsciously applied this strategy to all of my relationships, even after I got married.

Unpacked, I can see my trauma was holding me back from experiencing real connection and pleasure with my husband. I think it's expected, to an extent, when something like rape is involved. If I said anal sex became an "off-limits idea" for me, I doubt anyone would be surprised. Many women feel this way without being sodomized, so of course, I'd feel that way after what happened, right? But what if I told you I could never relax during sex of any kind? If I told you I didn't trust my husband because the men in my life before him betrayed me in such a profound way, you might feel less inclined to side with me. After all, he isn't them, which is something he has proven time and time again over the last decade. *Give the man a break, Andi!*

For the record, I agree. Doing this work within myself to figure out why my shields kept flying up hasn't been easy. It has forced me to dig up painful memories and less than flattering truths about myself that I've long kept buried. I treated my trauma like a trifling bitch I could just block, delete, and carry on without, but that's unrealistic. We cannot run from the traumas that have happened to us. I mean, we can, but they always catch up one way or another.

Think of it like the tortoise and the hare. Trauma is the tortoise, and we the survivors, are the hare. In the beginning, victory seems imminent. Running from those deeply rooted feelings and memories is effortless. *Peace out, pain! You can't outrun me.* The tortoise falls behind. So far back, in fact, we eventually forget about the race altogether. *I could really use a cheeseburger right about now. Let me pull out my carrot phone and see if there are any good spots around.* Since we've forgotten why we were running and what we were fleeing from, we begin to settle in for some sightseeing. *Oooh! Let me get a selfie with this cactus-shaped like Gumby!* Eventually, we travel so far off the racecourse, we run into other people, maybe even a suitor who becomes a life partner? *I'm a totally put together adult hare, and you're a totally put together adult hare, let's get married and make babies!*

Soon love, marriage, and the bunny baby carriage are over-flowing, and you're like, *"We need a vacation from this hectic hare life."* So you book a mini road trip with your hunky hare hubby and the two of you hop along merrily en route to your destination. On your way, you see something moving slowly on the gravel road that sparks a memory. *Oh, my carrots! Is that? No, no way. Could that seriously be?* The closer you get, the more flashbacks you have. You think it's impossible. After all this time, after all of these years, memories begin to race through your mind. Suddenly, you see the tortoise ahead of you as clear as when you left it on the starting line. You try to catch up, but it's too late. The tortoise lifts its long-clawed, webbed foot up and over the finish line seconds before you. Slow and steady, it won the race, and you bring your furry little paws up to your face in shame and disbelief. *But, I left you behind. How could I forget to finish the race?* You realize then, of course, that you didn't win, because you never finished. You simply got distracted from the world around you and forgot to continue on your journey. But the tortoise played the long game. It moved leisurely throughout the course without anyone to challenge it.

What the hell do I mean by that? Like I said, trauma is the tortoise. If we try to run from it, life will eventually distract us enough to fall behind it. And when that happens, trauma creeps up on us and slowly wins. It takes over our conscious mind and begins micromanaging all of our decisions, relationships, and emotions. It wreaks havoc on our hearts and kicks up loose gravel in our eyes. It plays the long game because it knows all it has to do, is outrun our efforts to avoid it.

I dodged my memories of Kyle and that season in my life until it finally caught up with me and threatened to win the race. It vowed to rob me of human connection, companionship, and trust in someone other than myself, but realizing this has allowed me to call off the race entirely. Instead, I, and I think all of us, must learn to walk hand in hand with the tortoise. Only then, when we not only admit to ourselves that it's a part of us but also, learn to stop running from it, can we experience healing. I'll never forget being sodomized and harassed by my high school boyfriend. It's a part of my story I cannot erase, avoid, or outrun. Living alongside it, instead of trying to run far away from it, offers me the chance to isolate the trauma as a single season of my life rather than a rulebook for men, relationships, sex, and love.

Allowing Kyle to ruin sex of any kind for me was an act of shrinking. It took unpacking to understand the reason I couldn't ever fully relax my body, even as a married woman. Our bodies hoard unchecked trauma, and it manifests in the form of physical pains or discomforts. I never considered how my experience may have been playing into the ways my body felt and received sexual connection before. Once I began unpacking, I realized I've held tension in my thighs and pelvis for years, sometimes making sex I dearly wanted to have with the man I love, painful and uncomfortable. When I finally recognized I was still living my life belly down on that bed, it was like a spark lit within me. *I won't let him continue to rob me of connection, consent, and climax.* Like Louise Hay articulated, "You have the power to heal your life, and you need to know that. We think so often that we are helpless, but we're not. We always have the power of our minds...Claim and consciously use your power."

I can trust my husband, my body, and myself. I can experiment in the bedroom and even have anal sex if I please because Derek isn't Kyle, Kyle isn't Derek, and I'm not my trauma. Sex didn't sodomize me, a person did: A snake in human skin that has long since been removed from my life. A person I've happily lived without yet tried to outrun for so long—too long. The only way out is through, and the only way through is together. The tortoise and the hare, side by side walking the course, slow and steady. Slow and steady. Trauma doesn't get the last word unless we freely hand it over and personally, I got tired of letting it sneakily have the edge on me in the wings of my life. Embracing my story stopped it from consuming me. It gave me permission to let go of the lie that I can't trust men because they'll never protect me. It gave me permission to let go of the myth that I needed a man's protection at all.

CONTROL: SO MAYBE YOU'RE NOT A CRAIGSLIST KILLER AFTER ALL?

*"A journey is like marriage. The certain way
to be wrong is to think you control it."*

— JOHN STEINBECK, *TRAVELS WITH CHARLEY: IN SEARCH OF AMERICA*

ON A BREEZY SPRING EVENING, AS THE SUN SLIPPED BEHIND
the hills with orange and pink hues following closing behind like a
wake trailing a harbor cruise, a lemon soared through the sky like
an eagle before attacking my right eye as if it were dinner. I was
standing outside of my friend Brett's house with a curly-haired
musician named Noah. He was a year older than I, and we were
unofficially, officially dating. He and I were playing Sandy and
Danny in *Grease* for a theatre competition and decided to take
our stage romance on the road the way so many actors do when
they spend several hours a day pretending to be in love. Noah
and I became adventure buddies of sorts, taking midnight hikes
to look at the stars and driving around our small town blasting
indie music from Osma and Jenny Lewis. That night, we found
ourselves outside of Brett's place to say hi and for some reason

in an attempt to be funny, he proceeded to chuck lemons at us until one assaulted my eye.

The lemon broke on contact and squeezed juicy sour magma into my eyeball socket. It burned worse than when the technician at the nail salon accidentally files your nail too close to the cuticle. The boys suppressed their laughter as well as they could, but that just made their faces resemble how one looks after too many plates at Thanksgiving. Air passed through their stuffed expressions, creating a whisper of giggles and Brett ran inside to grab some water so we could try to wash out the fiery hell juice from my eye. They both helped me flush out my eye as well as they could, and Noah and I got back in the car as Brett left in shame for what he had accidentally done to my poor little peeper.

Noah brushed the hair from my forehead and ran his fingertip down the side of my face.

"How's your eye feeling?"
"I think I'll live," I chuckled.

He lifted my chin and planted his lips to mine as we began to make lemonade out of lemons, kissing passionately under the fading sun. Things began to heat up, and before I knew it, Brett was moving my hand to his crotch. He, of course, was hoping to work up to what all senior high school boys wanted in the waking moonlight—some mouth to dick resuscitation. However, I was a young woman of moral and principle. At sixteen, I'd only touched one penis, and I most certainly had never brought any near my mouth before, nor did I intend to start that evening. They pee out of those things, and heaven knows teenage boys aren't using baby wipes to keep their dicks fresh. I politely declined the offer to his temple of doom, and shortly after, our romance had its final curtain call.

A few months later, Kyle told me he was thinking of killing himself, and we all know what happened next. He was the first person I finally experimented with, but it was out of necessity rather than desire. Since Kyle had a nasty habit of forcing himself on me, I'd learned from him that men won't continue to coerce you into sexual situations if they have an orgasm, so I began giving him blow jobs to keep his mouth away from my vagina. I rationalized this as a necessary action to keep my body from being defiled and to save myself the exhaustion of faking orgasms just to keep him off me.

After Kyle, I had the good fortune of meeting a nice Christian boy named Dean at my friend's church. I confided in him about being raped, and he confided in me about not really being sure that he believed in God. We talked for hours and quickly became boyfriend-girlfriend. I loved that Dean was from another town. I felt like I could be whoever I wanted with him. It was like a fresh start. He didn't go to my high school, which meant he hadn't seen me breakdown in the second period or heard the rumors around school about me. He saw the version of me I always thought I was: Pure, innocent, and beautiful. Or at least, I thought he did at the time.

I quickly learned that one of Dean's favorite things about me was how "experienced" I was. Never mind the fact that my aptitude was a result of rape and sexual trauma, Dean had never had a serious girlfriend before, and I was just the lady to show him the ropes. He wanted to please me too because he was a gentleman, of course, but I didn't want him anywhere near my downstairs, so I applied my keep away method. I gave him blow jobs as often as I could to keep the demons at bay, and it worked for a long time until it didn't.

One night, over a year into our relationship, Dean was ready for more. His pickup truck had a camper shell, and our new favorite pass time was parking in quiet neighborhoods with tall shrubbery and dimly lit street signs. There we'd spoon in the carpet lined truck bed to have deep conversations and steamy make-out sessions. That night, however, Dean had something else planned.

"I love you, Andi. And I just want to be closer to you. Anal isn't really a sin because it doesn't break your virginity, and we're going to be married to each other one day, so I think it's okay if we take things to the next level."

Then he tried to enter me without any lubrication, as I lay with my back to his chest in the cab of his beat-up pickup truck. My body pulsed with each gulp of air between tears and the moment he realized I was silently sobbing, he stopped. Dean panicked and pleaded, assuring me that he honestly had no idea I didn't want it too, and I wondered how that was possible after the countless hours we spent in the last year sitting on playgrounds in the dark talking about my trauma, my rape, my sodomy. But I didn't say that. Instead, I accepted his apology and let the relationship pan out for another six months or so before finally calling it quits. Then I was off to find another man to love me.

That evening with Dean opened my eyes to the fact that it didn't matter how long I was with someone or how much I trusted them, men were men, and eventually, they were all going to try to stick their dicks in me. Consequently, I began to look at blow jobs like a full-time job to keep dudes away from my body. I clocked in and out of this career path like my life depended on it because it felt like it did. They became my way of keeping an arms-length between me and any young man who may try and hurt me, physically or mentally. I harnessed their power, their ability to cripple a man and make him forget about all of the things he wants to do to you. I used them to my advantage throughout every relationship until Derek came along and unlocked my muzzled desire.

Derek was the first man in my entire life that I didn't want to lie to from the beginning. Whenever I couldn't escape a man's touch in the past, I'd give a gripping but quick performance to get them off me. Yet with Derek, I had a robust primal desire to feel pleasure from him. *Pheromones are real friends.* I didn't want to escape his touch: I actually tried to lean further into it. Exploring one another's bodies became a human connection that I was eager to experience time and time again. Blow jobs suddenly had an entirely new meaning and purpose in my life. They were no longer a tool of protection but rather, a gift of appreciation for this man I love, and I enjoyed giving them freely. I began to use them to express my desire, love, and admiration for Derek, and I sheepishly offered my body for him to please as well.

Sexuality, as I'd come to know it, was more of a skill of manipulation than an extension of desire and love. I never opened myself up to the possibility of orgasms being a regular occurrence because doing so would be releasing control, and life had taught me it wasn't safe to be out of control. Derek challenged everything I thought I knew. He dissolved walls that were coated thick with barbed wire and electricity. I was powerless against his affection, and it was absolutely terrifying for a while.

We were two young adults, navigating life between the sheets and in the world together. He took the time to study my body. He paid attention to my movements, sounds, and whether or not my toes were curled. Likewise, I became in tune with his pulse, his warmth, and his motions. I found myself fascinated by his body and the way it moved, both in and out of the bedroom. I studied Derek like he was the most important exam of my life. I suppose in a way, he sort of was. Determined to see what made him tick, not for my own gain, but for his, I realized that this had been my first relationship where I wasn't trying to have the upper hand. I didn't want to be the boss; I wanted to be a partner. I wanted to stand by his side. Only, I was struggling to renounce my power and ability to manipulate a situation with the touch of my hand, and old habits die hard.

Without weaponized blow jobs and fake orgasms in my back pocket, I was vulnerable, and I learned from my past that vulnerability in a relationship was dangerous. Since I wouldn't reboot these powers of mine, I searched for others to fill the cracks and help me stay on top so Derek couldn't hurt me like everyone else. Unfortunately, what I landed on was a cocktail of jealously, judgment, and control. I swore myself in as governess of house Derek and began enforcing laws that could be modified or changed at my discretion. It wasn't conscious, but my need to compensate for the control I'd lost in the bedroom was palpable, and I could feel the concoction rotting away my insides and sucking the life from the man I loved.

I became one of "those girls." I'd assume he was up to no good without any reasonable cause. I questioned everything and trusted no one, ripe in insecurity and thick in conspiracy theories. One afternoon I stayed home watching *The Craigslist Killer* on Lifetime while Derek was golfing with a friend and when he got back I was examining his sunburn lines and genuinely interrogating him because *what if he's a Craigslist killer and he was actually out with some girl who he had sex with and then murdered instead of on the grassy course at hole 9 working on his put?* I lived for passive aggressive comments about how he spent his free time and expected him to spend every waking moment with me. I'd feel anger swell up in my chest if he hopped out of bed in the morning to go outside and play with the dogs or work on the yard. I kept mental tabs of how long he played his video games and who he was playing with instead of sitting with me. I even chastised him for taking naps on the weekends, guilt-tripping him into staying awake by saying things like, *"Well, what am I supposed to do while you nap?"* The more intimate our sex life got, the more insane my thirst for authority became, but it wasn't until years later that I was able to connect those dots.

It was as if someone had tattooed the word "shame" on my body in invisible ink, and every time I had an orgasm, a black light would shine over the skin and show my mark. So in an attempt to cover it back up, I'd be grasping for straws trying to latch on to the first thing I could control, and well, Derek was always the closest straw to me. It was a game of deflection between the Devil on my shoulder and me. It was puppeteering my every move with whispers about how my sexual appetite was disgraceful. In the sheets, I could let go just enough to experience pleasure, but in the world, I was making up for that loss in control by projecting my shame onto Derek. But you can't heal a wound by pretending it doesn't exist and bandaging a different part of your body. Ugly bits of our hearts don't just go away. We have to face them and deal with them first, and I hadn't, so mine just drifted to a different location. I needed a slap in the face, a dunk in cold water, a lemon to the eye to wake me up and force me to see I'd merely traded one area of control for another and it was hindering me from experiencing true partnership.

UNPACKING CONTROL

When we've been hurt before, it can feel impossible to trust some-one again. It's an embarrassment of sorts for prideful folks like myself because it forces you to admit that your judgment isn't as good as you thought it was. It requires you to face that you're just a human being who makes mistakes, like everyone else. So many of us make excuses like, "I'm a great judge of character," but if we look into our past we can see where that opinion about ourselves we are trying to pass off as a fact is actually flawed. I struggled to accept the fact that I loved being out of control in the bedroom. There was a belief looming over my head that if I admitted how good it felt to let someone else take the wheel and steer me to ecstasy, then I'd make myself susceptible to an even deeper level of pain once he got tired of me and left. Also, it felt embarrassing to confess that something I grew up looking at as wrong was not only something I enjoyed, but craved. It was like finding out you'd been singing the wrong lyrics to your favorite song for the first time on stage, in front of a crowd, during karaoke night.

If you haven't caught on by now, I didn't write this book to glorify myself and show the world how awesome I am. I wrote it to demonstrate the messy truths of human complexity and how we can deal with our darkest demons if we're willing to call them by their names and face them. My need for control was a leech on my love life, bleeding it dry with each crack of the whip. I fell in love with Derek exactly as he was; yet I was trying to micromanage him outside of the bedroom to deflect from my own deeply rooted need to come out on top or have an edge up on someone at all times.

It wasn't until I began unpacking the big truth, "You never initiate sex" that I started to understand how significant control was to the issue. Having someone come to you with their desires is empowering because it makes you feel wanted, but going to them with yours is risky. *What if I tried to climb on top of him and he wasn't in the mood? What if he pulled away when I kissed him, or I couldn't get him hard, or he thought my attempts to be sexy were laughable?* Being out of control in the bedroom was easy because I was simply allowing Derek to fulfill his desires and anticipate and fulfill mine, but the fact that I never took charge was bleeding out into our day to day life and making me a judgmental and bossy partner. Could stepping it up in the bedroom and embracing my sexuality really be the ointment my open wound had needed this entire time?

I began noticing that on the nights where I took the initiative, even if it were only in a small way, I would wake up the next morning with a pep in my step, far less concerned about Derek's schedule and more self-praising of my efforts the night before. I felt strong, sexy, and empowered when I acted on my desires first rather than waiting for Derek and that feeling always trickled into the following day making me a much more at ease and pleasant partner. But as soon as the high wore off, I'd find myself right back at square one, feeling like my desires made me out of control and desperate to dominate something or someone in its place.

Can you relate? Have you ever found yourself talking to your spouse like they were your child and sat back to wonder why? Maybe your reason isn't sex-related like mine, but chances are if you're working overtime to control the people you love it is because you're trying to compensate for another area of your life where you feel out of control. It seems so obvious to say, and yet, it's probably one of the most commonly forgotten concepts, but when we take control of our own thoughts, feelings, dreams, and desires, we don't try to control other people's. It opens us up to experience greater connection because instead of trying to make everything go our way, we live in tandem with our partners; and as a result, we get to explore the world through their eyes, too.

Right now in your relationship, you may be harboring less than loving feelings for your spouse, and I'm not in it with you, so you may have legitimate reasons to feel that way. However, I'd like to encourage you to take some time to think about this person you chose to do life with. Has he or she changed since you fell in love or have your expectations of your partner altered? And if you find you're the one who has changed your vision for how you want your lover to be, then my question to you is why? Is there an area in your life right now that you're feeling lost, embarrassed, or ashamed of what you're trying to save face for by getting all bossy pants on their ass? How would you feel if your partner placed the same sort of stipulations and laws on you every time you wanted to go catch up with a girlfriend, read a book, or get your hair done?

I've learned from my own bullshit, if a partner is genuinely what you're looking for, then you need to stop trying to control everything all the time. The things I love are not all the same soul fillers my husband loves. He and I don't see eye to eye on every issue, nor do we express ourselves in precisely the same way. We're different personalities with different love languages and different day to day routines, and that's not only okay, but it's also fantastic. If I wanted to marry someone just like me, I would've hired a mad scientist to make a clone. Derek is highly intelligent without sharing all the same thoughts as me, and he's magnificently skilled in areas that I know nothing about. My value doesn't diminish by letting myself "lose control" in an intimate setting with the man I love, and neither does his if I'm the one taking the reins that evening. Control isn't a superpower: it's the kryptonite of marriage. There needs to be a natural flow of things between two consensual partners. Two who are in it to give and receive pleasure and connection—both in and out of the bedroom. That's where harmony exists and where love is free to grow as she pleases.

REJECTION: A GIRLFRIEND'S GUIDE TO NEVER BEING TOO MUCH

"I don't want anyone who doesn't want me."

— OPRAH WINFREY

IT WAS SEPTEMBER IN 2006, BREAST CANCER AWARENESS month, and my girlfriend Jess invited me to the Susan G. Komen Walk-a-Thon at the Rose Bowl with her and her family who attended every year. I didn't know too much about it, other than her mom was a survivor and Jess said they played movies on giant screens and had 24-hour snack bars. I always wanted to attend a charity walk, and this one seemed especially cool since it was an overnight event, so I jumped at the opportunity to join my friend. I asked my mom to borrow twenty bucks to cover snacks since I was eighteen and still getting my footing at this whole managing your money game and had managed to already blow through my last paycheck. After a lecture about how I need to be better with my finances, my mom shelled over the dough and Jess and I hopped in my used 2001 white, convertible Seabring, top down, blasting Ashley Simpson's "Pieces of Me" album as we headed west on the 210 freeway toward Pasadena. It was around 4 P.M., and we'd just hit the early evening pileup, so we were dancing in our seats and belting out all the words to Ashley's jams as we sat, stranded behind a slew of vehicles.

Up ahead, I saw a middle-aged man dressed in all black, on the side of the freeway. He stood tall, with an honest Abe style top hat gracing his head, which I found incredibly amusing. I began to laugh and point him out to my friend, but when I gestured my hand in his direction, he was gone. There was no off-ramp nearby, and the walls themselves must have been about twenty feet high, so the idea of him climbing over was frankly, impossible. A chill crept up my spine, and I couldn't help but think whatever I just saw wasn't human, at least not anymore. I wondered if it was a warning, a bad omen, or a sign of terrible things to come. As a result, my stomach was in knots over it for the rest of the evening. To top it off, my boyfriend Nick stopped returning my texts at around 6 P.M. that evening, shortly after he arrived at his friend Mike's house party.

My mom believed that Nick was my first love. He was two years older than me, with bold Italian features and a contagious smile that scaled his cheeks like a mountaineer on Everest. Even though he was only about a foot or so taller than I was, there was something about that smile and his deep-set eyes that drew me closer. Or, maybe it was the fact that my friend liked him first?

My best friend at the time, Beverly, brought me into her church to help with the youth group she led, and Nick was a leader there as well. Bev had a major crush on him, which she vocalized to me before I put a face to the name. I know how that sounds, and you're right to think I was an asshole for moving in on my friend's turf. I knew the lay of the land, the laws of friendship that state in permanent ink, "DO NOT REACH FOR SOMEONE

ELSE'S CRUSH." Still, the moment our eyes locked, I knew I needed him to be mine. I tried to ignore the siren call for the sake of my friendship, but I was sailing on a direct course to Nick, and him to me.

To make matters worse, he liked to hang out with Beverly's older brother and go shoot airsoft guns in an old abandoned apartment complex. Occasionally, Bev started tagging along and bringing me with her. The more time I spent around him, the harder it became to control my urges. I know I should've stepped out of the ring, or at least been honest with my friend about what I was feeling, but I did neither of those noble, mature acts. Instead, I secretly pined for my friend's crush and worked overtime to get conversations in with him without giving myself away as a lawbreaking citizen of friendship. I justified my betrayal toward my friend, telling myself if he liked her back, then he would've made a move already, seeing as they had known one another for a while. *Why should we both have to miss out on this great guy? It's not my fault they don't click, and he and I do.* I know, guys, I know. Grab your torch and pitchforks. In a way, I deserved everything that was coming to me. Karma, if you will, for discarding Bev's feelings when I should've been upfront with her. But this story is far from over yet.

One night after a busy hour of leading junior high fellowship, I hopped into my Seabring to head home, and by chance, Nick and I ended up side by side in our cars, stopped at a red light. I don't know what kind of succubus possessed me at that moment, but I gestured for him to roll his window down and then declared we needed to exchange numbers and hang out. I'd never been this bold with a guy before in my life, but I could tell that Nick was a little on the dense side. Since he hadn't been picking up on my hints, but I could tell he was interested, I decided to go for it.

We exchanged numbers and decided to meet up at In-N-Out to talk just as friends. For Nick, our meet up was meant to be two like-minded, opposite sex, young adults conversing about life, but to me, it was a date. While Nick was on this one-sided date with me, we ended up on the topic of what we seek in a significant other. My heart raced as Nick grew silent and studied my eyes like they were going to be on a test later. At that moment, I sent a prayer up to God. *If I'm supposed to be with him, please send me a sign.* I felt a droplet of water on my cheek, right on cue. Our long gaze broke as we both surveyed the evening sky. It was kissing our skin. The rain started slow but picked up speed, and before we knew it, we were drenched in its downpour. There we sat, two stunned, and soaked people on the cusp of something new. When Nick's eyes revisited mine, he looked as though he'd just seen a ghost.

"What?" I asked coyly.

But Nick couldn't answer me. Instead, he kept his eyes locked to mine and grinned with that massive, pure smile, and I wondered if maybe he'd prayed the same wish as me in that silence? As he'd tell me later, it turned out, he had.

From then on, we were inseparable. We spent the summer together, exclusively as boyfriend and girlfriend, watching Dodger's baseball on his parent's patio in the harsh season heat and making out in his bedroom until we needed a water break. I cheered from the bleachers at all of his softball games and watched with pride as he stole the show every time. We did family dinners and beach trips, and at night, he'd play his guitar while I sang along to the tune. It was everything I always dreamed of, and I didn't even care when my grandma told me he was too short for me. *Andi, if you're taller than him in heels, then he's too short for you!* Okay, you're five foot even, old lady. Whatever you say!

Nick wasn't a virgin, but he made the decision to be "born again," which is fancy Christian slang for pretending you never had sex. In turn, he never pressured me for anything. We never "went all the way," but we did pretty much everything else. It was refreshing to be with someone who seemed more interested in who I was than what I could do for them, but not everything was sunshine and Dodger dogs for us. Nick's parents were very Italian, and they adopted a European mindset toward their children and alcohol. Drinking in moderation was no big deal in their house; in fact, it was almost encouraged as a rite of passage. Before we met, Nick liked to drink with his friends, but I was a self-declared straight edge, and this posed a problem. At that point in my life, I was still convinced Coors Light was a gateway drug, but he wasn't. So that night when he told me he was headed to a party, I already knew trouble was brewing. I had this overwhelming sense that something terrible was happening as some of the kids we were hanging out blasting "Hey There Delilah" on the grassy lawn in the center of the giant stadium. I can't explain it, but I knew he was cheating on me at that exact moment. I could feel it in my bones. I walked the track all night with my phone tightly gripped in my palm, waiting for a text back that would never come.

In the morning, I gagged on that empty feeling you get after a night of food poisoning. My belly was churning as if the acids inside were feeding on the lining of my stomach walls. Something was very wrong, and my body was trying desperately to warn me, but it was too late to protect me. I pulled up to my house and saw Nick waiting for me on the curb. Palms sweaty, voice shaking, I climbed out of my car and walked over to him. We didn't hug, we didn't kiss. Both of us knew something terrible had happened, and something worse was coming. I sat there waiting for his confession, but it never came. Still, the words that escaped his mouth first pierced like a dagger:

"Andi, we need to break up. You're no good for me. I realized last night when I was talking to my friends, I've become a different person with you, and I don't like that. You're just too insecure. And you have a lot of baggage. You're a broken girl."

I was dumbfounded. I imagine I looked like a pet that had been abandoned during a move. I hadn't showered in 24 hours, and the fresh air had turned my locks into a frizzy mess. I was timid, scared, fragile, and raggedy. And the man I thought was going to be my future husband just labeled me as broken, as if I was glass and my pieces were threatening to slice his toes open or something. This was the same guy who, less than 48 hours prior, had his lips on my lips. He said, *"I love you, have fun!"* and now he was proclaiming, *"You're broken, you're insecure, you're no good."*

First, I begged like a pet left behind. I cried out, *"Please, don't leave me. I can change, I can be better."* But Nick didn't come to negotiate, he came to break my heart. *"You're a broken girl,"* he proclaimed. Then he left, and I gathered my shattered bits and went inside my house and straight to my room.

Nobody had ever broken up with me before. I never let them. I always had to be in control, be in charge, and have the upper hand. I thought Nick was a safe place. It never even occurred to me that he'd drop kick my ass to the curb. I was so unprepared.

Two months later, Nick came back when I received a Myspace message late one December night from him, apologizing for his words and asking if he could stop by my house. We talked, he apologized some more, and before I knew what was happening, we were back in each other's lives as if nothing had ever happened.

Only this time, I knew the rules. You see, Nick taught me who I was, who I am, would be too much for people. He showed me my dad leaving, my rape trauma, and my personality were all too much. My baggage was too heavy. So, I learned to be less.

He turned twenty-one, and I moved out of my parent's house into an apartment with Bev. I started playing the occasional game of beer pong with him and his friends and tried not to show my visible scowl over the watered down taste of those blue mountain brews. I laughed at all the right jokes and sat in the background, offering timely commentary as they played hours and hours of Call of Duty. I stopped texting him as much and let him chase me. I didn't get upset when he canceled plan after plan to go bar hopping with his friends. Now, I was precisely enough. I was exactly the kind of girl he wanted: *A woman who was chill and fun to hang around. Skip the drama and also don't be so clingy. Heaven forbid you enjoy me that much that you actually want to be around me. Be interested in me just the right amount and at the right time. Preferably when I'm horny and not with my friends or playing video games.*

Eventually, the rain of divine intervention stopped pouring over us, and Nick and I evaporated. This time, I was prepared to let him go. We sat at the bottom of my apartment stairs, and he nodded his head in agreement as I insisted we'd simply grown apart. There was a hug, a goodbye, and that was that. I sat there a while after he left, still a broken girl. Only now, I was much better at hiding it. I may have lost my first love, but I gained the Holy Grail: **A Girlfriend's Guide to Not Ever Being Too Much.** Written by men, for woman, the handbook would make it so that nobody ever called me broken again. With my new arsenal, I'd never be too much. Rather, I'd be exactly enough, and not a raindrop more.

UNPACKING REJECTION

I hate horror movies, but Derek loves them. In the spirit of compromise, we made a blood pact years ago that I'd suffer through exactly two, but no more, a year with him. My vivid imagination, paired with sensitive ears and an easily triggered pulse, make me the target audience for these films. I'm guaranteed to scream, jump, cover my eyes while simultaneously pressing my thumbs over my ears, and carry the nightmare from the screen with me long after the show is over. Watching scenes that make me more afraid of the boogeyman under the bed than my two small children are isn't my idea of a relaxing or enjoyable evening, but again, compromise and love and all that stuff. So twice a year, I put on my big girl panties and say hello to monsters like Freddy Krueger, Jason, Annabelle, and those creepy radioactive creatures from *Silent Hill.*

One of the classic traits of a horror film is the inevitable scene where a character has the opportunity to escape virtually unscathed but instead, chooses the dark, ominous hallway leading to the villain's lair or decides that running directly toward the chainsaw sounds will totally get the protagonist out safe and unharmed. It's the moment where everyone in the audience starts shouting at the screen, *"No! Don't go that way you fool!"* but of course the idiot does anyway because it seems characters in scary movies don't really want to live all that much or have some sick sense of adventure or whatever.

Walking through the events of our lives is a lot like being the young heroine of a horror film. Sometimes the answers to our biggest questions reside right in front of our faces. *"Hello, there's a door right there that leads outside to safety!",* but we can't see it because we're too freaking focused on the scene itself. Our memories play like the creepy hallway scene, but instead of taking the obvious way out, we choose the harder path because we're too distracted by the sights, sounds, and smells of our memories to spot that the answer is literally an unlocked door waiting to be opened.

My hallway moment was Nick sitting outside of my parent's house, proclaiming, *"You're a broken girl."* That's the story, right? It's where the armed maniac stalked the house, and instead of running away, I ran straight to him just two months later, open-armed and ready to be slaughtered. It's easy to make Nick the villain because he said something awful to me; plus, it's my story, so I can spin it any damn way I like to suit my needs. Only, that would make me the director, not the ingénue, and I definitely didn't direct this film as much as I've spent years of my life trying to script this shit. So here's the truth that I've uncovered: The rejection that really slew me wasn't Nick's; **it was my own.**

I allowed that curbside breakup to change the core of who I was. I allowed the opinion of one young man to dim my personality and my light. I mean, who's the real villain here? The guy that said some rude words or the girl who killed her inner self in some insane attempt to be more lovable? Now that's a plot twist M. Knight Shamalayan himself probably didn't see coming. It took me twelve years to see that there was an open door to my left the entire time, but I just kept walking toward the slasher soundtrack anyway. Nick didn't ask me to change. He didn't offer an ultimatum or agree to give our relationship another chance if I followed x, y, and z. I made the decision to alter myself all on my own, and the price I paid was years of squeezing my birthing hips into the mold I'd hand-carved for myself based on what I learned men liked and didn't like about women.

From then on out, anytime I felt rejection from a male begin to creep in, I'd reject myself, even more, to fit in, and keep the upper hand. This is a powerful revelation because even years removed from Nick and his words I was still allowing the echo of *"You're a broken girl"* to reverb through my eardrums and move me like a puppet on a string. Where once I was like an Ashlee Simpson song, vulnerable, raw, and honest, now I was living like a techno beat with no lyrics or depth. I was a good time and just real enough to avoid being vapid, working overtime to snuff out the broken bits that made me unlovable.

I thought I was removed from this time in my life once I got married because Derek knew the ugly stories of my past, and he still chose me. He'd heard about the Nick's and the Kyle's and the daddy issues and still wanted to do life with me. But I was taking on the role of the victim, massacred by insensitive words and actions from these men in my life, without taking any real responsibility for the way I responded to them. I'm about to quote Gandhi here at the risk of being a basic author because this is important: *"Nobody can hurt me without my permission."* [1] We've all heard different variations of this, but the message remains the same: I am in charge of how I react to the words and actions of other people. Every time I peel back another layer of my past in an attempt to better understand myself, I uncover a sliver of responsibility I've long avoided. This isn't self-blame, it's empowerment. It's saying, okay, these things happened to me, but they don't have to define me like I've been allowing them to do so. The actions and words of these people aren't a reliable representation of who I am as a person. I get to decide that, nobody else does.

I want to make myself clear here: We cannot control what others do or say, and sometimes others say and do things that have devastating, lasting impacts on us. Sometimes trauma brings forth an inability to control our thoughts, feelings, and even motor functions. I've lived with PTSD in my past, and more recently when I found one of my best friends lifeless in her vehicle and listened to the last air escape from her lungs (a story for a later chapter), so I'll neither downplay the weight of severe trauma, nor will I tell you that you've somehow given someone permission to hurt you when you're merely trying to survive. This isn't that, and that isn't this. I'm not a fan of generalization for the sake of trying to make a point more universal.

Additionally, I want to remind you that this is what I personally realized within myself. The same may not ring true for you in all areas, and that's okay. You're going to have your own journey, and the things you unpack may look different than the ones I have, as may your own discoveries. For me, what I've unearthed from my journey with Nick was my rejection of self. Recognizing this has offered me the chance to forgive myself for denying who I am and to realize that Nick's words were not the law, they were one immature dude's opinion of me at eighteen years old. In the words of Benedict Cumberbatch aka Doctor Strange, which means he knows everything because he can stop and travel through time: *"If you have an over-preoccupation with perception and trying to please people's expectations, then you can go mad."* [2]

People are like clouds: No two are the same, and everyone sees different things within them. To some, you may look like a brilliant unicorn; and to others, you'll resemble a swamp monster. Just like clouds, we shift with the atmosphere, but we cannot simply stop being a cloud. To do that would be to disappear from the sky entirely. Sometimes we can sway others into seeing what we want them to see, but it cannot last long term because like the clouds, we'll eventually change our form. The paradigm shift happens when we stop trying to will others to see us as we wish we were and begin embracing who we already are, who we're evolving into, and who we were always meant to be. It seems obvious to say, "You're not going to be everyone's cup of tea," but when it comes to relationships, don't we try really hard to be the flavor we think will receive the most love?

When I stopped rejecting myself, I not only gave my own soul freedom, but I also offered my husband a chance to meet the real me. The messy, clumsy, hilarious, beautiful, full of life and emotions and opinions, me. Suddenly I wasn't the villain or the victim, I was the smart bitch we wish existed all along who sees her way out and takes it. I was the one emerging from the horror, the screams, the perfectly cued music, ready to pen my tale of how I survived rejection, how I survived myself.

BETRAYAL: IN THE ARMS
OF THE VIRGINS

*Shame, blame, disrespect, betrayal, and the with-
holding of affection damage the roots from which
love grows. Love can only survive these injuries
if they are acknowledged, healed and rare."*

— BRENÉ BROWN, *THE GIFTS OF IMPERFECTION*

I LOST MY VIRGINITY TO A SOUL-CRUSHING ASPCA COMMER-
cial as my boyfriend Brady thrust on top of me. You know, the
one where Sara McLaughlin was singing "Angels?" The sandy
brown carpet had stains and a lingering stench from the frequent
urine and fecal matter, gifts his chihuahua Dixon would leave
around the house. I remember wondering when the last time he
washed his sheets was as I listened to Sara's voiceover tell me
that for just sixty cents a day, I could save these poor helpless
creatures from imminent death. He was gentle and respectful,
making sure I was as comfortable as one could possibly be while
experiencing the inevitable pain of deflowering amid starving
felines peering into my soul in the background. We were two

clumsy twenty-year-olds, the last of all our friends to carry the torch of virginity, eager to set it aflame, and crossover into the world of adulthood. Two short months before we weren't even sure a relationship like ours could work, but now we were branding each other's names into our lives forever in-between daytime talk shows, while his mom was pretending she couldn't hear us from the next room.

If you'd asked me a week before that afternoon if I thought I'd be losing my v-card anytime soon, I would've said, not likely. And if you'd asked six years prior if I thought I'd lose my virginity to the weird but popular-by-affiliation guy in Mr. Carson's first-period biology class whose plump towering frame resembled that of a linebackers, the answer would've been a big hell no. For me, Brady was one of those people in high school that you vaguely remembered and needed a yearbook to put a name to. But he remembered me, and for whatever reason, a few months before I found myself naked in his bedroom, I received an A.I.M. message from him out of the blue. If you're in my generation, then you'll remember A.I.M., but for the rest of you, it was how we communicated before social media and gifs took over the world.

I was minding my own business on the internet when a window popped up from a screen name I didn't recognize saying, *"Hey, what's up? This is Brady, from high school."*

At first, I thought he was an entirely different Brady, one who was my friend in high school that I actually had conversations with on A.I.M. but after a few minutes of chatting and him sending over his Myspace link, I realized I was, in fact, talking to a completely different guy that I barely knew. When I asked him how he got my screen name, his answer was all over the place. *"You gave it to me a long time ago. Or maybe one of your friends? I can't remember, but you like baseball and football, huh?"*

I let the issue go because in high school he was awkward, but now he looked like someone I'd flirt with at a party. Basically I thought he was hot. Eventually, he asked me out and decided we should meet at a sandwich shop we both loved called Philly's Best. For anyone who's never heard of Philly's Best, it's delicious, but it's also not a restaurant. It's more like a superior Subway that serves canned beer, cheesesteaks, and pizza fries. I showed up wearing a t-shirt and jeans because anything else would be way too dressed up for the tiny building wedged between a Dress Barn and a Little Caesars Pizza. Our conversation was filled with cringeworthy moments one would expect from two people who didn't really know each other in high school trying to catch up while also seeing if they were compatible enough to date. About an hour later, we hugged and went our separate ways. I didn't know what to think about the date, and he must have felt the same because later that night, he confessed he was concerned about our morals and beliefs being so drastically different. He was referring to the fact that I was a Christian and he was an atheist, but at that point in my life I was in a rebellion against church. Ultimately, I assured him that Christian was a loose term, so we decided to give it another go and see where it took us.

On our second date, Brady took me to the Santa Anita race track to bet on horses. We laughed, drank frothy beers, made trifecta bets, and decided that perhaps our brands of awkward meshed well together after all. It wasn't until our fourth date that he actually kissed me. If you haven't caught on yet, Brady wasn't exactly a wine-and-diner, but I was never the type of girl to need fancy things, and I enjoyed how casual we could be with one another. I came over for turkey burgers and the Dodger game, and as Kershaw pitched, Brady turned to me and paused.

Always one to read the room, I could tell he was working up the courage to kiss me, and I opened my lips invitingly while I eagerly waited for him to make his move. We sat there through three strikes as Brady's inner monologue began to pour out of his expressions, and I watched him move his head back and forth as if he were weighing his options. Finally, he raised his eyebrows and his mouth curved into a grimace as if he were biting into a lemon in a "Fuck it, I guess I'm going to do this" kind of matter, and he kissed me. The entire approach was a bit off-putting, and I wondered if he was kissing me because he wanted to or because he assumed that was fourth date protocol. But he told me I was the most beautiful girl he'd ever seen, and I was desperate to believe him. So after that night where he marveled over my soft lips and glimmering eyes, I never left his side.

I became the trophy on his arms, proudly displayed at house parties and baseball games. Only, I didn't fit in with the other walking prizes, and I quickly became aware that I was more like one of those participation awards all the kids get just for showing up while the other girls were the first placers. All of Brady's friends were the jocks from our high school, and their girlfriends were younger, former cheerleaders with bleach blonde hair and perfectly smooth, tan skin. They all wore a size zero which they made sure I was well aware of and had been partying since they were thirteen. Meanwhile, I spent my teenage years in the theatre drinking Diet Coke and eating my weight in Taco Bell burritos. I was entirely out of my league around Brady's gang of tightly knit friends, and I was continually trying to figure out how to blend in as the black sheep.

One night after a day of watching football with my new crew, I curled up next to my mom on the couch and began to cry:

"I'm not like them, mom. I'm not beautiful like them. They're so put together. So pretty. So girly. And I wear blue jeans and tee shirts."

She sympathized with me, and I wonder if my insecurities stirred up her own twenty-year-old pains because the next day she took me to Sephora and we let an employee fill our bag with the best perfumes, highlighters, bronzers, and eye shadow. We went shopping, and I found a cute top and cardigan to wear for the BBQ that afternoon.

I showed up, the new me, but nobody noticed. The bronzer, perfume, brightly colored blouse, eye shadow, and highlighter didn't translate. I wondered if I was standing in the shadows of the sun. Maybe the light wasn't hitting my bronzed cheeks? Perhaps they weren't standing close enough to tell that I smelled like a daisy now, instead of whatever budget perfume I could find? I'd traded in my drug store makeup and my Kohls' clothes, and still, nobody saw a difference. And when I excused myself to the bathroom and looked into the mirror at the golden-hued eye shadow on my pale skin, I suddenly felt ridiculous. Still, I let new me stick around for months and years to come.

The new me was so much cooler than the old me because she could keep up with the guy's beer for beer and look cute doing it. She loved sports and booze, but she also wore wedge heels to softball fields and drank mudslides from coffee cups while she watched her popular in high school boyfriend run bases with his other popular in high school friends. I was in for the first time in my life, yet I'd never felt more alone.

Our connection began to crumble about the same time it did with Nick—when Brady turned 21. His birthday was a whole six months before mine, which meant I was no longer the most beautiful girl in the world but rather, dead weight. In early September, his best friend Steve invited all of his buddies and their girlfriends on an all-expense-paid trip up to Crater Lake, Oregon for his dad's wedding. Steve's dad was loaded, and he went all out for the event, renting Greyhound busses and stocking them with booze, and putting two couples each in pop up trailers all around the property. I'd never been to Oregon and was excited, so I wondered why the pit of my stomach was churning in knots the morning we left.

Brady didn't seem very thrilled that I was going to this weekend adventure he invited me to, and you could cut the tension with a knife as I stepped out of my car that morning with my small suitcase in hand. It felt like he was hoping I got into an accident on the way over or slept in and missed the bus. I tried to shake the feeling off as nerves since I'd never done anything like this before and proceeded to get drunk off whatever anyone would hand me on the eight-hour party bus ride.

When we arrived in Oregon, the vibe changed, and I was feeling hopeful. We barely had time to drop our things off in our trailers and change into bathing suits before a man with shoulder-length blonde hair and easy eyes had us all hop into his van. He offered us pot as he drove us up a long, windy road that led to the top of a giant river. There, we grabbed rafts, filled them up with beer, and began an afternoon river float.

The float was fantastic. With each twist and turn and cold beer, I felt more and more comfortable and sure that I'd merely been creating problems in my mind. But once we were off the river and my legs hit the dirt, I could feel it again: The river of resentment for my presence. Less than a week before we were mapping out our remaining two-year college plan and discussing where we'd live together, but now Brady could barely even make eye contact with me and every-time I'd press to try and find out what was wrong, he pulled distantly farther away.

The wedding night came, and I took my time curling my hair and painting my face with the other girls before slipping on a short strapless floral dress and heading to the outdoor venue to watch the "I dos." It was a beautiful ceremony, and the party was even better. There was an open bar, but since we were at an actual venue, they were checking I.D.s, and I wasn't twenty-one yet, which meant Brady had to get my drinks for me. But he kept disappearing. While his friends pulled their girlfriends in close during slow songs, my date was nowhere to be found.

I made my way over to the bar with Steve's little sister Ashley, and we played off the whole, *"Oops! I totally left my I.D. back at our campsite"* act well enough to land us two White Russians. There was karaoke happening on a large stage lit by hanging lights, and I finally found Brady sitting three rows from the front with a few of his friends. I went to sit down next to him, and suddenly the D.J. called out, *"Brady, come to the stage!"*

He leaped from his seat and ran to the stage, grabbing the mic and calling each one of his friends, and their girlfriends by name to join him. There was only one name he seemed to miss: mine. I sat there in the third row from the front as I watched all of these people sing Garth Brooks' hit "I've Got Friends in Low Places" and suddenly felt completely sober in this beautiful oasis as I realized that I didn't belong to Brady, or these people, or to anybody. A few days after we got home, he confirmed what I already knew. It wasn't too much thinking, too high of an altitude, or too many White Russians, after all. He was pulling away. A week before, he wanted to spend every single waking minute with me, and now he was saying he thought it would be best if we saw each other less. Space was the dagger he threw. He felt we needed space.

"I don't want to break up; I just think we should spend more time with our friends and less time together."

"But you're the one who always has me come over even when I suggest we take a night off or something. I'm just confused because this seems out of nowhere." I replied.

"You just...you love too much, Andi."

I could sense by the way he said it that he was trying to open my eyes to everything that was wrong with me. It was as if he thought telling me this truth would tone me down, and we could go back to when I was calmer, cooler, less vulnerable, and less in love with him. I wasn't sure how to process this new revelation that I "loved too much," but I also wasn't ready to let him go. So I agreed to space and let him call the shots. Instead of spending more time with our friends but maintaining a relationship like he'd claimed he'd wanted, Brady began screening my calls and direct messages. He started canceling plans, alleging he was busy while I knew well and good he wasn't.

One night, we had plans to meet up after his softball game (I stopped being invited to those), and he never showed. I tried to call, sent texts, and admittedly went a little (okay, a lot) crazy when I drove to the local pizza joint he and his buddies frequented after games and saw him look at my phone call, put his phone back in his pocket, grab his frothy beer mug, and say something to his friends before they all burst out into laughter. I'd become the punchline. The running gag. He'd grown tired of displaying me on his mantle and tossed me in a plastic bag along with the rest of the junk he was looking to donate. Rage and hatred were consuming me from the inside, but I couldn't find a way out of the misery. His claim on my virginity tethered me to him on a shrinking rope, and I could feel it tightening around my neck, but I couldn't find the strength or courage to cut it. I'd given myself to him in a way I'd never done before, and now he was acting as if I were some weird girl who slipped love notes into his locker in school and made up a fantasy about being in a relationship with him or something.

The fact that my twenty-one year old, recently ex-virgin boyfriend wasn't seeking me out for sex was a big red flag that something sinister was going on here. Men don't suddenly take up a pledge of celibacy a few months after biting into the apple; and in my heart, I knew the fact that he wasn't sleeping with me could only match up to one reality: He was cheating on me.

My best friend Alwyn was single at the time and had been fiddling around with a new dating website called OkCupid when suddenly she shockingly came across a face in her feed of local potential men that she recognized; my boyfriend. When I confronted him about it, he lied and said he only made a profile to mess with his buddy who had created one. Never-mind the fact that his "fake page" had a profile pic, location, age, description, and he'd taken the time to fill out all of the quiz questions. Alwyn and I devised a plan to catch him in his lie and created me a profile on the website in hopes he'd stumble upon it. If he viewed my profile, the site would inform me, and it'd prove he was actively using the account he claimed was only a hoax.

Hopeful, horny, young men immediately started messaging me, but I either ignored them or told them I was in a relationship. One guy who seemed nice enough, named David, was curious about why someone in a relationship would be on a dating website and I filled him in on the saga that was my life. He offered his friendship and advice, which I gladly took. One tip he suggested was that I do whatever I needed to do to uncover the truth. So I did what any girlfriend looking for dirt would do: I snooped.

It was around six o'clock on a Tuesday evening, and Brady made plans to go get ice cream with me, but when I tried to get ahold of him to confirm a time, he wasn't answering my calls or text messages. I turned to my computer to find him on A.I.M., so I sent him a message, but he iced me. He forgot that he'd given me his passwords and there was a gut instinct in me that knew I'd find my answers in his email, so I logged in and instantly felt my heart drop to my feet. He had at least three dating profiles on different websites. They all showed that he was looking for "casual encounters," and I read some of the graphic, grotesque messages he sent to girls before closing the window. I decided to log into his Facebook next, where I unearthed a message he sent another girl we went to high school with, and immediately felt like puking. It was the same *"Hey, what's up? It's Brady from high school, you're so pretty"* line he'd approached me with seven months prior.

My eyes were too stunned to leak as I sat cross-legged on my bed in front of the screen filled with my boyfriend's lies and betrayal. I finally understood what Sara McLaughlin was trying to tell me that afternoon when I lost my virginity to the commercial with her malnourished animal friends. I was drowning in the endlessness. The lies and wreckage she sang about as I locked eyes with a fading tabby kitten on the screen that I honestly think began crying in the exact moment I was unborn. She was trying to warn me. Her, the kitten, the scent of stale urine and dog feces. They were all trying to alert me. This is dangerous. You're going to feel lost. Wrecked. Lied to. I was the damn kitten all along, desperate and needy and begging for a $.60 daily donation or five-dollar Philly cheesesteak for affection. I didn't care if it was stolen, or borrowed, or blood money as long as I was fed.

I sent an S.O.S. to my bestie and right after, messaged David to see if he wanted to hang out that night with Alwyn and me. Then I got dressed, did my hair and makeup, made myself smell like a daisy, hopped in my car, and drove to Brady's house. I grabbed a softball he'd left in the backseat of my car and walked up to his driveway.

Batter up.

I knocked on the door.

Strike one.

I could see from the kitchen window that he was sitting at his computer in stained basketball shorts, his long fingers actively typing away. He was probably planning his next booty call with someone from any of the three or more websites where he was creeping.

I knocked again.

Strike two.

The door swung open, and I stepped back to let him move out of the door frame a bit, before hurling the softball at his chest.

Strike three.

"You're the grossest, worst person I've ever known, and I never want to see you again. FUCK YOU!"

Brady looked confused, which only fueled my rage.

"Don't you say a damn word. You know exactly what you've been up to, and now, I do, too. I saw it all, and I'm done. This is done. We're done!"

He tried to follow me out to my car to talk, but I was obviously far past the point of conversation and much more in the realm of, throw a fucking softball at your cheating piece of shit face, and he quickly realized he was caught, defeated, and done.

You're out!

That night, I drank Smirnoff Ice and made out with David on lifeguard tower 13 at Huntington Beach while my best friend walked the sand. Hating Brady, as it turned out, was fantastic. I lost eight pounds in a week on a strict, alcohol only diet, and I was meeting all sorts of guys on the internet who thought I was beautiful. I spent the next two months getting drunk, being drunk, going on dates with random guys, and attending any and every party around so that I could drink and flirt with more random guys. I was getting really good at being new me. I wore high heels, and bronzer, and smelled like a daisy, and knew to never again show another living soul the young woman I once was. I recommitted myself to the teachings of **A Girlfriend's Guide to Not Ever Being Too Much: Written by men, for woman** and worked overtime to ensure I'd never be the broken girl or the one who loved too much again. I was doing the damn thing, dating around, refusing to be tied down, until one evening when I got a message on OkCupid from a guy I was sure must have messaged me by mistake because he was way too hot for me. A guy who looked like something out of G.Q. magazine and seemed to be hilarious, based off his profile. His name was Derek, and I couldn't know it then, but the moment I hit reply, my life would never be the same again.

UNPACKING BETRAYAL

Is anyone else beginning to think my relationship patterns are a lot like the song that never ends? *Yes, it goes on and on, my friends.* If you've ever felt like Bill Murray's character in the movie *Groundhog Day* when it comes to relationships it's because we accept the love, we think we deserve, and a lot of us don't think we deserve all that much. It's not conscious, at least, not entirely. I think deep down I always knew when I was in a bad relationship, but I was seeing these men as who they could be instead of who they were and that's why I let a lot of the unsettling actions slide. We make excuses for others when we're looking for affection and conclude that it's better to have mediocre love then no love at all. Unfortunately, it's that approach that often leads us into the lion's den to be devoured.

What I learned from my time with Brady, was the rumors about men were correct. They only want one thing, and once they get it, they want it from someone else. This breach in trust made it difficult, moving forward, to accept that maybe not all men are created equal. Since I'd yet to see any hard evidence supporting the claim that good honest young men existed, I walked into the next chapter of my life jaded and continuously looking for cracks in the pavement. I became hyper-focused on finding something wrong, so I could validate my theory about men. Through unpacking, I realized I was still holding on to an edge of this page I ripped from the handbook, even though I was now married to a man who was in fact, kind and honest.

The truth I unearthed from revisiting the story I'd been carrying about my time with Brady, was that he and I weren't compatible. I was trying to fit a square into a circle, but the only way to do that was to shave down my square until it was small enough to wedge in. We didn't believe in the same things, but instead of taking that at face value, I declared I'd be different than who I was to make it easier for us to work. By the time I was chucking a softball at him, I didn't know who I was any- more because I'd betrayed that person to be with Brady and now Brady was betraying me. It was like double jeopardy. How could he be convicted for the crime when I'd already committed it on myself first?

You may be noticing a reoccurring theme in this book by now. If you're anything like me, it may not immediately sit well with you. Taking responsibility for my place in each scene of my life hasn't been easy, which is why I spent years avoiding it entirely. But that's also why my marriage was missing a key component: Me. **All of me.** It wasn't until I started doing the uncomfortable work that I realized I was still holding myself back. I was afraid of being betrayed again, and in the process, I was still betraying myself. Not allowing yourself to experience love at its fullest capacity is the ultimate betrayal, and I was found guilty when I took the stand and put myself on trial.

Maybe my love was too much for a guy like Brady. He clearly wasn't really looking for love in the first place, but that didn't mean it would be too much for everyone. As long as I continued to allow his actions and my betrayal of self to hold a claim of me, I'd never be able to give my love fully to anyone because there would always be a giant chunk of it hidden away in storage. When you're zoomed in on all the reasons someone may break your heart, you tend to miss all the reasons they won't. My husband loves me. He chose me and continues to choose me daily, which is why I needed to finally pardon him from someone else's sins and stop treating my marriage as if it were founded upon a mountain of quicksand.

Friends, I want to clasp my hands over yours here and tell you that good men and women do exist. If you find yourself in their midst, in their beds, in their hearts, do yourself and them a favor and don't make them pay for someone else's transgressions. If someone from your past betrayed you, don't take the memory of that betrayal and in turn betray your new partner, or worse, yourself. Our history isn't our master, it's a teacher. And it can be our most excellent teacher if we lean in close and listen to it. In the words of Otis Redding, you've got to "try a little tenderness." Find comfort in the arms of your spouse, in the arms of yourself. Free from the wreckage of those who hurt you before, and open to give and receive the love you have always deserved.

COMPARISON: STEPPING OUT OF THE SHADOW

"Comparison is the death of joy."

– MARK TWAIN

I'M ONE RESOURCEFUL MOTHER FUCKER. IT'LL PROBABLY BE etched on my grave.

Here lies Andi Franklin
Wife. Mother. Resourceful Mother Fucker.

My survival instincts aren't the ones that will win me any awards. I can't make a fire from dryer fuzz, disarm a hostile person, or run for more than ten minutes without getting side pains and convincing myself that I'm probably going to have a heart attack and die. I've got no idea what plants will heal me and which ones will seep into my skin and eat me from the inside. *Seriously, don't let me around plants because I'll probably kill us all.* The only time I ever had success with anything botanical was the witch potions I concocted with my cousin when we were younger to make the neighbor boys fall in love with us because we were bored and that's what kids did before cell phones. You'll never find me on a survival challenge show because I'm addicted to lip balm and unable to cope with mass amounts of ants being within five hundred feet of me, but I'm really resourceful. I find solutions to problems, look outside the box, and work with what I've got. It's the reason my husband won't volunteer me as a tribute during the zombie apocalypse, second only to the fact that we may be responsible for repopulating the earth, but I digress.

What I lack in skill, I make up for in resourcefulness, which was a vital talent to possess when I first met Derek. I'd only ever slept with two other guys before I met him, and both of those were within that same calendar year, so I was still learning what it meant to arch your back while my steamy new boyfriend had been arching backs for years. I was a novice at best, straight-up terrified amateur at worst. But Derek? He'd been around the block. He was hot and experienced and oh-my-god he's going to realize I'm just a loser drama kid and dump me. So, I turned on my resourceful-mother-fucker hat and learned how to fake it till I made it so far into his heart that it was too late for him to turn back because of my lack of sexual experience, knowledge, or even basic skillset.

Operation trick him into thinking I'm a goddess was implemented by food. I may not have known what reverse cowgirl meant, but they say the way to a man's heart is through his stomach; in essence I figured if I could satisfy his literal appetite, then it would compensate for any way I may have been lacking in the sexual appetite department. I started easily with a spaghetti recipe that I practiced at home first before bringing my bag full of ingredients to his apartment to impress my new boyfriend and his roommate with a homemade marinara sauce Ina Garten would be proud of. Only, I made the mistake of assuming two college dudes had basic spices and materials such as sugar, and thus my marinara never reached its full potential like it had when I rehearsed it at home. Cooking quickly became a part of my love language for my new beau, and without realizing it, I began relying on food to do a lot of the heavy lifting for me in the relationship to compensate for everything I felt inadequate about in my own self.

One morning I got it in my head that he was mad at me for whatever reason, so I made the hour drive to downtown LA to get bagels from his favorite spot, and it ended up being closed—indefinitely. So instead, I googled the next best place around, hand-selected a dozen, and drove all the way to his beach apartment to drop them off on his porch. I wrote on the box, *"Sorry for being a bitch."* When I went to leave them, the door was open, and he was home playing video games with a friend. So I did what any sane person would do: I crept around like the Grinch who stole Christmas, sliding the box on his porch mat before running to my getaway car like a teenager who just toilet papered a house. When I was safe inside my car, I sent him a text letting him know there was something at the door for him before sheepishly driving away. One, he genuinely had no idea why I called myself a bitch and didn't have a clue as to why I thought he was mad at me. And two, was super confused as to why I ran off like he was the boogie man or something.

Here's what he didn't understand then, and what I could never tell him: I'd learned from my past relationships what guys wanted and who they wanted, which was a woman who was chill and fun to hang around. Skip the drama and don't be clingy. Heaven forbid you enjoy me that much that you actually want to be around me. Be interested in me just the right amount and at the right time. Preferably when I'm horny and not with my friends or playing video games. And me being the resourceful mother fucker I am, found a way to master that role. Every once and awhile I'd slip and show my insecure side, and that's when I'd bust out gestures like the great bagel bitch excursion of 2009.

I've got to say, Derek must have really loved me, even then. Because in my attempts to seem like a normal, chill young woman, I probably came off as a total basket case. And yet time and time again, he'd hug me, love me, and show me that he wasn't going anywhere, even though everything I'd learned from previous relationships cautioned me he'd most likely drop my ass to the curb. I worked overtime to keep my flaming feelings for Derek at bay because neither he nor I anticipated being in a serious relationship at that point in our lives and I was terrified if I let him all the way in, he would hop on his noble stead and get the hell out of town. In another act of resourceful mother fuckerness, I treated myself like some homemaker/call girl hybrid, often coming to his apartment to cook or have sex and then driving home before bedtime.

One night as I zipped up my knee-high black boots and pulled rogue locks from my head, reframing my face, Derek sat up in his bed and waited for my eyes to meet his.

"Why do you always get up and leave?"

The question took me off-guard. *"You've never asked me to stay before."*

"You're my girlfriend, and you live an hour away. You think I expect you to drive home? I just assumed you knew you were

invited. It never crossed my mind that you wouldn't stay until you kept leaving."

I hadn't considered that me showing up and leaving like some sex-seeking thief of the night might actually make Derek feel uncomfortable, or as if I wasn't as committed to the relationship as he was. That night I could see in his eyes that he was genuine in his efforts to pull me in deeper to him, so I stopped making myself a booty call and instead took on the role of a partner. After that night, he couldn't get rid of me even if he tried. We were obnoxious. We talked all day and spent almost every evening together. Definitely, all weekends were reserved for each other. It was blissful and fairytale-like, and I was always waiting for the other shoe to drop. And when the shoe never fell, I'd periodically grab it and chuck it across the room for good measure. Because Heaven help the wicked, nothing gold can stay, all good things must come to an end. But Derek, he was like a revolving door: Every time I pushed, he'd come right back around faithfully.

Still, l found myself standing on my tippy toes all the damn time. I never put two together, but the truth was I'd become a master of manipulation, both toward myself and my partner. I was forever downplaying my insecurities by making myself overly accommodating. I would anticipate a problem and solve its imaginary self before anything had ever formed. (Bagels, you guys.) I felt so unworthy of Derek's love that I spent every waking minute trying to prove myself to him. He didn't actually need proof that I was the woman he wanted, but I sure as shit did. I felt possessed to show him I could be what he deserved, and in the process, I put myself through hell to do it and gave an inner angry mob speech if I failed.

She's a loser! (A loser!) And she'll never be worthy! (Unworthy!) We can't sit by and let her pretend she'll ever be happy! (Cue the crowd in my subconscious making various sounds of agreement).

In the early days, Derek and I were both terrified of falling into one another. He was fresh off a Euro trip where he prowled his way around twelve countries, healing his heart after the end of a four-year-long relationship, and I'd recently been cheated on by the guy who swiped my virginity. Basically, we were both two twenty-one-year-old shit piles that had no interest in love or relationships and just wanted to celebrate our single lives and have some fun. But fate had other plans for us.

I still remember our first date like it was yesterday. I actually had plans to meet up with another guy after dinner with Derek on that breezy November night. Derek will tell you that I was a half-hour late to the restaurant that evening, because I'm sure that's how it felt when he thought he was being stood up by this girl he found on the internet. Still, I maintain that I walked into the restaurant closer to ten after five and it was love at first sight. I know how outrageously cliché that sounds, but I knew right then and there as he led me to the outdoor table he had already selected, I'd follow him anywhere, and it scared the living day-lights out of me. I couldn't eat my dinner because my stomach was rolling nervous knots, but I did drink two beers because I needed all of the liquid courage I could muster.

I felt like Gidget when she realized she was in love with Moon doggy, and if you don't understand that reference, do yourself a favor and go stream it now. *Gidget* is one of my all-time favorite films, a regular tomboy dressed for the prom, boy talk about an American classic! My mom introduced it to me when I was younger, and we'd watch it on repeat. There's a scene where

Gidget asks her mom how you know you're in love and she describes, *"It feels like getting hit over the head with a sledge-hammer,"* and when I walked toward Derek, Cupid came swinging at me in full force. WHACK!

When he invited me to go grab another drink somewhere else, I said, *"I'll follow you anywhere."* I mean, I didn't because that would've made me seem like a psycho, but I thought it as I concocted a cool, calm, *"Sure why not?"*

We ended up at a college bar near the ocean with handcrafted beers and shuffleboard tables lining the back wall. The chemistry between us was kicking up more dust than the discs we were sliding back and forth through the sandy game table, and after a while, Derek mentioned he planned to meet some friends at another spot and asked if I wanted to join him. You already know my answer. *I'll follow you anywhere!* But I was cool.

"Sounds fun" (Code for: marry me now).

I excused myself to the restroom where I proceeded to cancel my second date and text Alwyn who was supposed to meet up with me and second dude, that the plan had changed and she needed to get her ass over there to meet my future husband. That night we met each other's best friends. I took free tequila shots with a stranger, bought a pitcher for the group, and we cuddled up as if we'd known each other for years. The date lasted twelve hours. We both knew right then and there what we'd accidentally stumbled upon, but the timing felt so wrong. We weren't prepared to settle down again; neither of us. Yet, we also weren't ready to lose one other. So, at the risk of falling, we jumped in, hearts first. We teetered, and we fumbled, and the only fact we held back from one another was our undying love because neither of us wanted to seem like a lunatic and declare such bold feelings so early on in the relationship.

Like most new couples, we spent time talking about what life looked like before the other came into it, spending hours chatting about our pasts and our recent heartaches. I told him about my long line of unreliable and hurtful men, and he recalled his long term relationship and where it went wrong. I was intimidated by the length of time he'd spent with his ex-girlfriend Emily because it more than doubled my longest relationship, and I'd never personally experienced extended commitment like that. I learned a lot about her, partially because he felt comfortable being open and frank with me and partly because I asked an absorbent amount of questions; but the more I learned about her, the more I let my insecurity take the wheel. Emily's family was wealthy and well known in the city, which meant when Derek was with her, he got a lot of perks like meeting celebrities and attending VIP events. All my family had to offer was crippling debt and a frozen yogurt punch card. Everybody knew her before they knew me, so I felt like cubic zirconia trying to replace a diamond. I saw his ex as this giant shadow looming over me, and had built up a version of her in my mind that painted her as "the one who got away," branding myself as a solid runner up or consolation prize.

The imaginary version of Emily I formulated was perfect. She smelled great, always looked put together, and wore sexy lacy lingerie around the house while she cleaned. She exuded confidence. She was smart, funny, tall, and tan. I pictured her opening up her own puppy orphanage and drinking nothing but kale smoothies for glowing skin. Imaginary Emily never complained or felt lost; and instead, she paraded through life with a sultry smile tattooed to her face and always got what she wanted. I spent eleven months imagining all sorts of elaborate reasons why Emily was superior to me, and then the unthinkable happened, and I ran into real life Emily on my twenty-second birthday.

It was past midnight in a crowded, two-story bar, and she made eye contact with me across the room before charging toward me like a Trojan horse. The confidence, just like I'd envisioned. It was almost closing time by then and I gave her my best Lucy Ball face of discomfort, but she charged on. Noticing I was her clear objective, I turned my back, hoping it would deter her from making contact. Not a minute later, I felt a tap on my shoulder.

"I know this may be awkward, but I'm Emily, Derek's ex-girlfriend."

Oh, hell. She was towering over me in her heels and flattering floral print dress. She was an Amazonian goddess with glowing tan skin just like I anticipated. Suddenly, I was deeply aware of my hatred for the abstract white and black blouse I was wearing. I could feel the acne pulsing on my face. My hips felt as if they were bulging out of my jeans, and I wondered if it was the booze goggles, or if she really was as flawless as she seemed. I managed to utter out a quick hello before Derek jumped in for damage control. Only, I was an insecure drunk girl meeting her boyfriend's ex on her birthday, so as he casually caught up with the Amazonian queen, I slithered into the background and disappeared. I rushed to the bathroom where I tried to convince myself that everything about me wasn't atrocious, and when I returned Derek was waiting for me at the bottom of the stairs, ready to rescue me from myself.

I played it cool because, remember, that's what I did! On the walk home, I laughed through my discomfort and tried not to make a scene about what had just occurred with the night queen. We ended up having sex on someone's car in a small ally about a block from our apartment and declared our drunken undying love for one another before heading inside to get some sleep. The next morning was Halloween, and as Derek hopped in the shower to get ready for the day, I logged into my Facebook and found a message waiting for me from Emily.

She wanted to apologize for ruining my birthday, citing she heard from a mutual friend that I was very upset. She needed me to know that she was a great person who cares about people and that she'd never intentionally hurt someone like that. Then there was some bit about being in a similar circle and not wanting to have any discomfort between us, and an offer to get coffee if I wanted to chat. I'd been found out. She looked right into my half-open, bloodshot eyes and saw right through me. I felt naked on trial as I read her words, as if the car I fucked on the night before was blasting its high beams on me and the ally was a courtroom.

Where were you on the night of October 30th, 2009? Is it true that you shrunk into nothingness upon meeting your boyfriend's ex? And is it also accurate that you're aware you'll never be good enough for him? Are you prepared to walk your stubby legs in her giant shadow for the rest of your life? ARE YOU? Answer the question!

I sat in bed in the apartment Derek and I shared together with our roommate, laptop and shaking hands in tow. It was time to put on my resourceful mother fucker hat, to fake it till I made it. I knew how to do this: I was good at this facade. I'd been doing it my entire young adult life. The reply needed to sound confident, level-headed, and kind. Maybe sprinkle in a touch of "I don't give a damn" for good measure?

This is what I managed to reply:

"Hi, Emily! (Note the exclamation point which is a giant red flag that I was trying too hard to come off like I didn't have a concern in the world about her swooping back in to claim her ex from me.)

Sorry if I came off as mean last night. I'd been drinking since 7 P.M. and was pretty drunk by the time we met. LOL. I don't have any thoughts toward the type of person you are. What happened between you and Derek is in the past and is none of my business. I'm sure we'll see one another around (hell, Derek and I live right by all the bars!) and that's totally fine with me. Despite what you may have heard, we had a great night last night, and I hope you did, too. Happy Halloween!

Andi"

I read and reread my words before hitting send. I felt confident and cool, and definitely positive that I was the mature, kind one of the two girlfriend gladiators. I'd used my skills to seem like a woman who was chill. Fun to hang around. Skip the drama. And also, don't be clingy. Derek and Emily would both be fooled. I'd played my first Halloween trick, and I was basking in the satisfaction that I'd pulled it off without a hitch. Only, I still felt her shadow looming over me. Subtle, but there. Refusing to get out of my spotlight. Refusing to let me shine. Tapping me on the shoulder from behind and confidently barging itself into my life.

"I know this may be awkward, but I'm Emily, Derek's ex-girlfriend."

Awkward? A little. Soul crushing? Absolutely.

UNPACKING COMPARISON

Sure, Emily seemed like a literal giant, towering over me with her naturally tan skin and wide gleaming hazel eyes. And sure, I felt like I was a tiny ant in front of the Statue of Liberty when our paths crossed and she so confidently raised her torch above me and declared herself known. But in truth, she was never the giant, my giant that I needed to face. The Statue of Liberty was given as a sign of peace and good fortune. Why, then, was I so overwhelmed by her placid presence? Why did she feel so big and bold and intimidating?

It's simple: Emily was a symbol, just like lady liberty herself. She was a monument of my insecurities that I needed to brave. When I saw her standing her ground, I admired her. I wanted to be like her. To have this unwavering, untethered belief in me, like she did. I don't know if she approached me to hurt me, to prove that she was an adult, or because she genuinely just wanted to say hi, but what I took from it all was that this young woman in front of me was fearless, and that terrified me. I wondered if it was because she felt prettier, or smarter, or more capable than I was. It felt as if she was sending me a message that I was all the lesser for walking in her shadow, and it triggered the very worst parts of me that I'd worked so hard to bury.

Emily forced my resourceful mother fucker into a ditch. She slit me wide open with her dagger eyes and shoved the cool chick in me down into a dark, muddy hole filled with worms, and roots, and rot. Suddenly, I was utterly exposed for the person I really was rather than the person I was pretending to be, and it was mortifying. I grew obsessed with trying to convince myself and especially Derek that I was still this level headed woman, but it was no use. The gig was up, and I'd been caught. Found out.

My insecurity and jealousy snatched up my body and took hold. They grabbed a shovel and piled pounds of loose dirt over my once cool persona, and when they were done, they left the grave unmarked so that no one would ever stumble upon it again.

Not surprisingly, walking around with your skeleton completely exposed is alarming. I was suddenly acutely aware of just how rigid everything was. A breeze blew like a tornado, a ray of sunshine scorched like a third-degree burn. Moving one foot in front of the other felt so tricky without all the muscle, tissue, and blood to cushion the bone. I couldn't find my usual responses to uncomfortable situations anymore because they'd been buried, and I was entirely unable to hide. You could spot my fear, insecurity, and shame from across Times Square.

I could feel myself drowning in the harsh waters of the Atlantic, treading for dear life in the statue-shaped shadow reflected in the water, but it was like I refused to paddle from the shade and toward the shore. I think Emily became an excuse for me to doubt myself. I used the role she played in Derek's life as justification for my own lack of confidence. One of those, *"Of course I'm insecure! How could I think highly of myself when I have to follow in the footsteps of someone like Emily!"* type of things. It was easier to blame Emily than to admit I simply didn't think I was good enough. The truth was, I would've felt that way whether there was an Emily to follow or not. At the end of the day, I didn't believe in myself. I didn't think I had anything worth offering. I saw myself as this damaged, baggage filled girl who loved too much, and I was looking for any excuse to look outward for the cause of my probing problems.

Comparison is like tree sap, sticking to anything and everything it touches. When we feel uncertain about who we are, we cling to outside sources for approval, validation, and justification.

We cannot expect people to tiptoe around our insecurities, especially if we're working overtime to mask them like I was. I allowed my own fears of inadequacy both inside and outside of the bedroom with Derek to fuel a vigorous comparison game that Emily never asked to join. She couldn't help but be exactly who she was, and it wasn't up to her to play small around me, so I'd feel more comfortable. It was my job to put the chess piece down and stop trying to prove to an invisible force that I was a formidable opponent in a game nobody was playing, but me.

In retrospect, when Emily tapped my shoulder and declared herself known, she gave me a glorious gift. Shattering my resourceful mother fucker into pieces was exactly what needed to happen for real me to come out. And once I was forced through the threshold, I found not only was I not as terrible as I assumed, I was actually pretty damn great. I'll never have long legs or a natural tan, but I'm fantastic just the way I am, and Derek already knew that. I just needed to catch up to the party. I was comparing myself to the ghost of my boyfriend's past, but all I needed was to look inside and let the real me have her day in the sun.

I've come to find it's only when we relieve ourselves of the duties of comparison that we can tap into our own power and let the light within us shine. Comparison clouds our hearts and makes us small, but acceptance for ourselves empowers our souls and breathes life into our hearts we can then pour out into our relationships. There will always be an Emily. Whether she's an ex-girlfriend of your spouse or someone on social media you can't stop stalking and comparing yourself to, the Emily's of this world will always exist, and most of the time they'll have no idea what their presence means to you. We're in control of how we allow other people's existence to make us feel about ourselves, and frankly, other people are none of our business.

Maybe Emily takes extravagant family vacations across the world? Maybe her house is immaculate, and she looks like something out of *Elle* magazine on a Tuesday morning grocery run. Perhaps she hangs out with Kevin Bacon on the weekends, and they both discuss how everyone can trace a story back to them thanks to their wide range of work and friendships. Possibly she dines with royalty, farts glitter gel pens, or eats her cereal with gold flakes in it for vitality and healthy gut flora? Maybe she's everything I dreamed up in my head, or maybe she's just another normal woman with her own battles of insecurity, self-doubt, and comparison? Whatever the case, it's none of my business, and it has no effect on who I am and whether or not I am worthy of love.

Let me repeat and rephrase that for a little extra emphasis: The woman you're comparing yourself to is none of your business and has no effect on who you are and whether or not you're worthy of love. Comparison is poison, but the good news is the antidote already lies within you. So grab the chessboard and toss it out the window. Light it with a match and throw it into the fire. Bury it along with whatever fake version of yourself you're hiding behind. Because at the end of the day, you can't cook, clean, smile, or fuck your way into loving yourself. That has to come from you, by you, for you. And it's nearly impossible when you've got a mask on and an Emily under your scope.

BODY-IMAGE: THE PIZZA PANTRY PUZZLE

"To lose confidence in one's body is to lose confidence in oneself."
— SIMONE DE BEAUVOIR

DEREK PROPOSED TO ME ON MY TWENTY-THIRD BIRTHDAY. HE convinced me we should throw a lavish murder mystery party since my birthday was on a Saturday that year, and I was born the day before Halloween. I love birthdays —capital "L" LOVE them! Birthdays are special to me because they're a day devoted to telling someone how happy you are that one exists on this planet. I love them —as long as they aren't mine.

After my biological father Kevin left a week before my 7th birthday, I convinced myself as the dreadful day approached each year that the people I loved would ultimately decide I wasn't worth their time anymore, just like he did. I grew to hate the "all eyes on me" aspect of a birthday, fearful that more attention would only heighten the level of pain I was sure to experience. I preferred to be the celebrator, not the celebrated. It felt safer to treat my birth like any other day of the week; so I deemed anyone who cared about me during that time like a terrorist to my heart. I made a habit of pushing people away from me the closer it inched to October 30th, convinced they were going to leave me anyway. I figured if they were going to split, I might as well give them a real reason. You know, an excuse other than the one I was most afraid of; that I simply wasn't lovable.

By this point, Derek had already survived one birthday with me. As you may recall, it involved a confrontation with his statuesque ex that threw me into hot mess Medea mode. I didn't understand why, but he was committed to my brand of crazy and also to this whole "Let's have a big bash!" idea, so I reluctantly agreed and let him take care of all the celebratory details.

He chose a murder mystery package called, "Murder of a Millionaire" which was themed around Rick Rochester, a (you guessed it!) millionaire who mysteriously died. Rick's dying wish was to have a party thrown in his honor, where the reading of his will would also take place. Apparently Rick didn't trust people much in his life either, because the guest list included his ex-wife, pool boy, nosy servants, and anyone he thought may try and gain from his death. My friends and family arrived dressed to the nines in costumes varying from a crisp white chef's jacket, to Derek's grandmother donning a sexy maid costume, since we were using her house and amenities for the party. I played the role of Jasmine Rochester, Rick's current wife, and now a widow.

If you've never participated in a murder mystery party, you're missing out on balls to the walls fun. They're so entertaining and are perfect for spicing up a regular party and pulling people out of their comfort zones. It's like a live action version of the game, Clue, with adult beverages and fun costumes. I'm telling you, try one. They're so fun and even your people who claim they can't act will find themselves lost within the fourth wall the moment the plot heats up. And it always heats up in a murder mystery party, because about halfway through the game, there's a murder. *Dun, dun, dun!* Then participants are typically given an envelope with new information about their characters and whoever was murdered gets reincarnated as someone new who was fashionably late to the deadly bash.

That evening when I opened my post-murder envelope, there wasn't anything about my character inside. Instead, I found detailed instructions from Derek to sneak out of my own party and go on a scavenger hunt throughout his grandparents' generously sized house to locate my surprise birthday present.

Earlier that day, Derek insisted I go and get my nails done with my mom, which is something he'd never done before. I had an inkling he was proposing, but as I sat in the salon chair, I told my mom I was abandoning the thought because I didn't want to get my hopes up and ruin the night he'd so thoughtfully planned for me. But now I was on a wild goose chase through the house, and a tingly sensation was rippling throughout my entire body. The riddles eventually led me upstairs into his grandparent's room, where their dumbwaiter was.

I opened the door and found a folded piece of paper inside. Immediately I thought, *"We must be taking a trip somewhere, and that's where he will propose!"* but the second my eyes hit the first word I knew the moment was upon me. Printed in italics was a declaration of love, commitment, and instructions to sneak outside to the gazebo. Tears were already falling as I crept downstairs and made my way to the front of the house where the gazebo was suddenly illuminated with twinkly lights. Derek stood in the center waiting for me, and as I turned the corner, I noticed he'd propped up a framed photo next to him.

It was a picture of me and my grandma Lucy, who died two years prior.

"I know you wish she could be here for this, and now she is."

He took my hands, got down on one knee, and spoke.

"I know your birthday has always been a day of pain for you, but I want to change that. I promise to always be your light in the dark. I hope that from this moment on, your birthday is a day of celebration. You are the greatest person I have ever known, and I promise to love you, far longer. Will you marry me?"

I barely let him finish before shouting "yes" and pulling him up to kiss and embrace. Cheers came from behind; and when I turned around all of our party guests were lined up holding a plastic pumpkin with a letter carved out, spelling, *"Will you marry me?"* It was everything they claim in the movies and more. A borderline disgusting, beautiful display of not only Derek's love for me, but his demonstrative attention to who I am.

Like most newly engaged women, I got straight to work. We decided pretty quickly that an October wedding would best suit us, and everyone told me I needed to push myself into a bridal boutique to get a wedding gown as soon as possible. In turn, my mom, a few of my bridesmaids, and I booked two appointments for me to try on dresses. I said yes to the dress in the first store we went to, and the owner took my measurements and filled out the order form for me to sign. Leading up to my visit, I was advised that wedding dresses run small and to expect mine to be a size or two higher than my "normal." So I was stunned when the owner decided my dress would be a size 4 when my usual size was a 6. In fact, I even mentioned it to her, but she insisted she was basing it on my measurements and felt the four was my match, so I trusted the professional and spent the next several months waiting patiently for my dress to debut.

When it finally arrived, I was called in to do a fitting. I was beaming with joy as I pulled the dress up and over my thighs, but my enthusiasm left as quickly as it came when I realized I couldn't get the damn garment over my butt. Frustrated and a little emotional, I decided to try the overhead approach. This worked wonders for me in the past when my big booty got in the way, so I pulled the heavy gown above my head and shimmied. I was able to squeeze myself in, but barely. I called my mom in for back up and then walked out to the platform where the mirror was for the owner to lace me up and make her adjustments.

"It's pretty snug in the butt area," I whispered.

She tugged on the dress to get it in the correct position, began lacing, and inquired:

"Have you gained any weight since your fitting? You know, it's pretty common for brides to start eating salads and exercising more, so they fit better in their gowns."

I was mortified. I hadn't gained a pound, but my dress barely fit, and now I had this callous woman accusing me of eating too many brownies in my free time and recommending a salad diet and fitness routine. Perhaps a reasonable person would've been able to write this off as the owner making a mistake from the beginning by ordering me a smaller size? Maybe someone more confident would've given her a piece of her mind for insinuating

I needed to lose weight? But I wasn't an average person. She was talking to a twenty-three-year-old woman with a longstanding case of body dysmorphia, and she sent me spiraling with her one backhanded comment about salads and exercise.

The Mayo Clinic defines body dysmorphic disorder as a mental disorder where one focuses obsessively on his or her perceived flaws, which can often be non-existent, minor, or undetectable to the outside world.[1] In my case, BDD showed up in the form of me seeing my body two times bigger than it was at all times. While I've never been formally diagnosed, my therapist in high school noted my symptoms and suggested I consider additional care for it, but I never did. High school was hard enough after being raped, so I couldn't also admit I'd developed an eating disorder. My pain threshold was maxed out and besides, how right could she be? After all, I didn't have the physical appearance of someone with an eating disorder. I wasn't stick thin, I didn't throw up my food, and aren't all teenage girls obsessive about what their bodies look like? Still, being unable to trust your own eyes really screws with your brain, especially when someone casually drops a "You should probably lose a few pounds" bomb on you in a store lined wall to wall with promises of happily ever after. *Happy only for the women who can fit into a size four, apparently.* I started exercising for the first time in my life and calling a piece of fruit a meal. And when no one was watching, I began the vicious cycle of closet eating.

One evening Derek ordered a pizza for dinner, which is my favorite food on the planet. Pizza was crafted from the heavens and delivered piping hot and fresh from the head honcho upstairs himself, I'm sure of it. If it were up to me, pizza would be served at every event for the rest of my life, and I'd fall to my knees in gratitude for its cheesy goodness. However, back then, I still labeled food as "good" or "bad," and pizza fell into the seven sins category. I pinched myself off at two small slices and longingly dreamed of more for the next hour or so until I couldn't take it anymore. Derek had slipped off to the bathroom, and I saw a box of opportunity.

I crept into the kitchen and pulled a slice out from the fridge. It felt sexy and dangerous pressing the buttons on the microwave to re-melt the cheese, and I was careful not to let the timer reach zero, so that the buzzer wouldn't blow my covert operation. I sunk my teeth in and felt an instant rush of satisfaction hit my brain, but just as quickly panic set in as I heard Derek shuffling around down the hall. He was out of the bathroom, so it'd be mere seconds before he walked in on me and my cheesy adultery, but I couldn't let that happen. He couldn't see me like that. I frantically scanned my surroundings, trying to find a place to hide the evidence. I was running out of time, so I threw the paper plate holding my slice of pizza in the pantry and moved away from the crime scene to conceal my gluttonous crime.

Derek walked into the room and didn't miss a beat. *"Did you get more pizza?"*

In my pursuit for melted cheese, I hadn't considered that microwaving the slice would re-introduce the smell into the air. I looked bashfully at him before shaking my head side to side like a toddler with applesauce stored between his or her cheeks, but he wasn't buying it.

His voice grew loud and excited, like a treasure hunter on a new crusade. *"Are you hiding it?"*

He began excitedly searching for the slice, opening drawers and cupboards and growing more eager with each glance at my panicked face. I tried to change the subject and direct his gaze toward the living room, but he was on a mission. Then the moment he locked eyes with the pantry, it was game over for me. He stretched out his arm, opened the door, and gazed upon the open tomb in shock and disbelief. There it was, a slice of pepperoni pizza on a flimsy paper plate sitting on a canned beans pedestal.

Derek combusted with laughter, and I stood there, trying to find a way to explain myself, but all I could think of was the bridal boutique owner and her words. *You know, it's pretty common for brides to start eating salads and exercising more, so they fit better in their gowns.*

I cried silent tears in the bathroom that night, pushing my stomach out to make the bloat more dramatic and seething with hatred for my bagel buns. Why were my arms so full? Why were my breasts so small? Why didn't I have enough self-control to fix myself? I honestly hated her, that undisciplined, pizza smuggling woman staring back at me with her pale skin and big hips. I was so ashamed to be her. To live in her acne-prone skin and shimmy skinny jeans over her stretch-mark-kissed thighs. All I had to do was eat kale and get on a treadmill, but I couldn't stop myself from sabotaging it. I didn't deserve to fit into my wedding dress. Who was I trying to claim a seat in the "happily ever after" section of the room, anyway? My ass was too big to fit in those tiny chairs. I took up too much space: I was always taking up way too much space.

With habits like this, it should come as no surprise that I didn't lose a single pound before my wedding day. I chalked it up to genetics, but the truth was that for every soggy salad and half-assed HIIT workout I did, a version of pantry pizza awaited. I'd practically starve myself all day, and by dinner when my body couldn't handle the hunger anymore, I'd cave. Derek would leave the kitchen, and I'd package up leftovers, spooning extra servings of rice into my mouth straight from the pot or eating warm pasta from the Tupperware I'd just packaged it in neatly. Every morsel of something that wasn't dieting culture friendly was treated like my last supper. I'd stuff myself until I felt sick, chanting "this is the last time" over and over in my head. Then, the shame would boil over and I'd spend the rest of the evening pulling at my non-existent stomach fat. My inner monologue would start her speech about what a failure I was, and the cycle would start all over again in the morning.

It was an exhausting way to live. A sad one too, because there was absolutely nothing wrong with my body, only my mind. I was exerting myself trying to fit into a gown when it was my head that needed to drop the weight. It was always my thought patterns with the problem, but I couldn't even see my body and that was on the outside, so how could I fathom what was going on inside?

UNPACKING BODY IMAGE

I chose this story to talk about my self-image, but I honestly had dozens more to pull from the bag. There's no shortage of incidents for me when it comes to this topic—no single event that stands out in my mind as the worst but rather, the collection of them all that shows me the dark hole I was dwelling in for so long.

I've pinpointed the start back in middle school when I had those icy blue metal frames on my face, skunk streaks in my hair, and more fat on my body than any of my friends. Back then it was fashionable to decorate your school folder with glamour photos of your friends and family, along with pictures of bands and singers you love. Mine donned magazine clipping of N'Sync, 98 Degrees, some mall photos of my girlfriends, and some pictures of my family including one of my older stepsister Brittany in her swim team photo that she autographed and gave me.

I always wanted an older sister, so when my mom married my stepdad Karl (who I call "dad" in real life but only refer to as "stepdad" in this book for clarification) and combined our families, I was over the moon to inherit her. Britt didn't share my enthusiasm, but I really can't blame her. She was an only child being thrown into a growing family, and suddenly she had a little shadow following her around the house and copying her every move. She may not have been ready to have someone idolizing her inside the home, but she was undoubtedly used to the attention. My sister was a mix of Brittany Spears and Jessica Simpson, with long blonde hair, blue eyes, perfectly sun-kissed skin, and the body every girl dreamed of. I knew my sister was a knockout, but I never felt jealous of her until one day in P.E. class.

We sat in the large auditorium with our belongings gathered, ready for the bell to ring when one of the popular boys next to me noticed my folder full of pictures. He slapped the picture of Brittany in her royal blue school bathing suit and exclaimed, *"Who's that? She's fucking hot!"*

For some reason, I took pride in his remarks about my sister. Of course, she's hot. She's the prettiest girl I've ever seen, and she's my family. That makes me cool by association, right?

"That's my sister! She's gorgeous."

The boy looked up from the photo, then back at me, as if he were trying to solve a riddle:

"That's your sister?! No way. There's no way. She's way too hot to be related to you!"

"Well, technically she's stepsister, but...»

He cut me off sharply.

"Ohhhh. That makes sense then. I was gonna say...»

He didn't have to finish. I hadn't pieced it together before, but when I heard his tone and saw his expression, I knew that I was the ugly stepsister. Before that moment I was just me, but after, I was something else. When I looked in the mirror, I suddenly cared about my bushy eyebrows and squinty eyes. I noticed that I was the only girl in my group of friends whose thighs rubbed together when they walked. I became acutely aware of my otherness.

So despite shedding the baby weight in high school, getting my eyebrows waxed, and ditching the glasses, I still saw that awkward little middle schooler sitting in the auditorium, realizing for the first time that other people thought something was wrong with her —with me. This is when I stopped relying on myself to determine my confidence and began looking outward for it. I couldn't trust my eyes to tell me if I was cute or a socially acceptable size or anything because they'd deceived me into thinking there was nothing wrong with me when boys obviously thought otherwise. There was a deep level of distrust for my own self that I believe led my brain to create a version of me and my body that reflected how shitty and unloveable I felt on the inside.

Inside, I was trying to fit these massive lies into a still-developing prefrontal cortex. It was like my brain was a broken-down carnival ride; and suddenly I saw everything through the lens of a funhouse mirror. I was distorted. I'd no idea what I really looked like anymore, and so I became obsessed with trying to understand. I sought outside approval for my appearance at all times. "Does this make me look fat?" "Can I pull this off?" "I really need to go on a diet." To be in my life meant to sign up for a validation committee where you'd be subjected to millions of critical comments about my appearance but try and maintain composure amid the barrage of body shaming, even if others weighed more than I did. I never considered how I was making others around me feel because I didn't see anything wrong with them like I did with myself.

I need to take a moment to explain this illness a little more, because I know how it comes off: *If this bitch thinks she's fat, then she must think I'm a whale!* No. This isn't about you or anybody else. BDD is an obsession with your own appearance, not others. Even then, I never looked at other women and boxed them in like that. There was no size meter determining their worth in my brain; it didn't work on anyone else's body but my own. I could find a million beautiful traits about any woman who crossed my path, but I looked at my own self with utter disgust. I didn't understand how my negative self-talk was affecting me, so I certainly couldn't see how I was impacting the people around me either. I never contemplated the message I was sending a friend who weighed more than me or even one who just struggled with body issues like me when I made callous remarks about my appearance. I was entirely tone deaf. Even when I could feel the people around me getting tired of my shit, I couldn't stop. My body felt like the greatest mystery of my life because I had no idea what it really looked like and I desperately wanted to explore it.

In retrospect, I've let my weight, pant size, and ab definition determine my worth for as long as I can remember. I cycled through high school, my 20's, and even the beginning chapter of my 30's staring, pulling and prodding every inch of my flesh.

Some may lie awake at night thinking of ways to organize, or planning for their day, or watching porn—but, me? I've spent hours combing the internet for "before and after photos" of other women with similar body types as mine for "motivation"—or rather, like some sick form of punishment for not being at their level. I've hired personal trainers, drank meal replacement shakes, gone vegan, given up sugar and alcohol and caffeine and comfort and grace and joy. I've dabbled in keto, paleo, clean eating, high fat, low fat, no fat, good fat, and everything in-between. I once got so sick from the cabbage soup diet that I had to quit halfway through—but not before losing three pounds in three days eating like a rabbit trapped in a human's body. I've cried over ice cream cravings, sulked over wine not being "diet-friendly," and have gotten so sick of sweet potato that I could barely put it in my mouth without wanting to vomit.

I've also missed out on life. I've gone out to dinner with friends and refused to eat. *Sorry, I'm on a diet. You enjoy it, though.* I've ditched opportunities to spend quality time with people because I was too worried about missing a workout. I've sulked in a lovely restaurant for my cousin's baby shower and watched everyone eat delicious looking sandwiches and salads that I declined because I'd already eaten the food I brought from my home, four hours away, in my car. I genuinely cringe when I think about that last one. Did I believe a turkey avocado sandwich was going to turn me into an orca? Was I that insecure, that vain, that lost? Yes, I was.

Of course, I cloaked it under a different name: *This diet isn't vanity or insecurity; it's determination and self-restraint! Look how marvelous and healthy I am!* That's where the demons lurk, and danger lingers in the "look at how great this is!" while slowing dying inside. The "check out my bikini bod!" cheer while sobbing into a container of cookies I'd been sniffing in hopes of tricking my brain that I'd cosmically consumed them.

If I couldn't handle social settings without my body issues getting in the way, it should come as no surprise that my marriage suffered from them as well. I couldn't even climb on top of my husband without quickly turning around because I was embarrassed of my body. I'd never have sex with the lights on, fuck that. If he rubbed his hand across my waist while walking past me in the hallway, I'd freak out like he was going to discover I was smuggling an endangered owl under my clothes or something.

All I wanted was to feel confident in my own skin, to feel sexy and desirable, but I was trying to fix the wrong parts of myself. It was like there were two puzzles laid out in front of me; one completed, and one in pieces. And instead of working on the incomplete puzzle I kept ripping the already done one apart and rebuilding, as if the pieces would suddenly fit together differently and form a new picture. Derek would chime in all the time hoping to help me see there was nothing wrong with my body, trying to get me to work on the other jigsaw, but I brushed him off anxiously. *It doesn't matter that you love my body: I need to love it, too.* Technically, I was right, but I'd never find that love until I made my way to the other puzzle. I didn't need to fix my body: I needed to fix my mind. It was my insides that needed a crash diet, not my outsides. I needed to trim the fat from my brain that was clogging it and leaving me foggy.

Nobody ever told me that loving myself would be this hard and I'm guessing I'm not alone because the diet industry was estimated to be worth 72 billion dollars in 2019 according to Business Wire,[2] and it continues to increase. Let that sink in for a hot second: $72 billion was generated from our combined insecurities, insanities, and desires to be healthier. There's a new juice cleanse, fast, meal replacement shake, pill, wrap, food restriction challenge, and so on popping up daily. The popular verbiage that sparks people's interest these days is diet masking as a "lifestyle change."

Let me make something hydrated-pee-clear here: Nourishing your body with whole food and regular exercise is vital for your mental and physical health. When I see someone take control of their wellness by moving his or her body and listening to its cues for food and hunger, I do a happy dance: *Yay, you!* There's nothing wrong with wanting to be healthier, or stronger, or even to want to feel more confident on the beach. The issues reflect in the methods we are being fed to try and achieve these goals. We're all so desperate to be an overnight sensation like so-and-so who "lost 60 pounds in two weeks" that we stop listening to our bodies and frankly, put them through hell. The industry is setting us up to fail because, of course, they are. *Dolla Dolla bills, ya'll.* If fasting, or juicing, or eating less than 1200 calories a day, or not eating chocolate ever again, or hermit crabbing in our houses for the rest of our lives so that we don't have to be tempted by social settings or the world, in general, were sustainable methods of weight loss, then the damned diet industry would go bankrupt overnight.

The truth is that there's a giant boardroom somewhere filled with lavishly wealthy men and women. I picture them business on the top, Lululemon on the bottom and all they do is sit around an oval table eating cake with 24k gold flakes and laughing maniacally at me, at you, at all of us. *Jason just snagged another 2,400 people with his "fast guide to weight loss!" And Shelly's new 72-hour detox tea sold out in 20 minutes! With the relapse rate climbing every minute, we're already on track to hit over $80 billion this year, and it's only January!* Then everyone cheers, and they get burgers and fries, and salads and milkshakes delivered, and everyone gobbles what sounds good to their bodies because they all know the 72 billion dollar secret: Diets are bullshit.

They're the O.G. false prophets of our time, my friends. They promise us big triumphs like a tiny waist, abs, lifted butts, and worthiness. *You'll be so worthy once you're thin! Look how worthy you'll be!*

I've looked good in a bikini and still felt disgusting. I've hit my goal weight and still agonized over my thighs. I've gone over the schematics of my calories in vs. calories out that day in my mind while my husband is on top of me trying to connect. I'm here to tell you that true confidence doesn't exist in a pant size. You won't discover it in a meal replacement shake or a dairy-free, gluten-free, nut-free, meat-free, sugar-free, air diet. You won't find it in the food you're eating or in the food you're not. Worth cannot be found here in Dietland. And if your obsession over your appearance is causing you to miss out on truly connecting with your spouse and even the other people in your life, then it's time to start working on the personal piece of the puzzle. Because confidence, true confidence, cannot be found in a measurement. And I can promise that if you don't love you now, you won't love you then either. No matter how good you look in a bikini.

Friends, if you're hungry and tired like me—eat and rest. Reevaluate your relationship with food and reacquaint yourself with the living definition of health and wellness. If living doesn't fit into your "lifestyle change," then you may want to take the blinders off and really look at what you're doing. Is this sustainable? If I died tomorrow, would I be proud of the way I spent my last day or would I regret not meeting up with that friend for lunch or having that glass of wine on the balcony with my husband? Stop looking at life as some marathon you get to jump in and out of as you please. Tomorrow doesn't exist yet. It has yet to be determined. It may come or it may not, so how do you want to live today?

Eat the salad that leaves you feeling fresh and just the right amount of full. Go on that walk or do that circuit training that calms your mind and makes you feel healthy. But don't sit in your car crying outside of Wendy's drive-thru because you want a frosty, but you're "trying to be good." Don't fall asleep at your desk because you're on day 3 of this juice cleanse, and you "really want to lose 5 pounds." Don't put your body and your mind through the ringer and call it wellness, because it's not. It's a joy-killing hell that you'll yo-yo in and out of for the rest of your life while suits in Lululemon eat the cake you're crying over because they know the 72 billion dollar secret.

Diets are bullshit. And once we realize this—once we really understand that our bodies and minds are unique and powerful and worthy of being trusted—then we'll find freedom. Freedom to discover what works for us. Freedom to break away the shackles of restrictive living in the name of "health." Freedom to live our lives in true wellness, both mentally and physically.

You can get the body you dream of by doing something extreme, sure. But at what cost? Are you willing to keep it up for the rest of your life to maintain those results? And do you truly believe that will bring you the self-love you've been seeking? The other option, of course, is to allow your body to show you where it feels best. To give a big middle finger to the scale and realize that number doesn't define you and it doesn't determine your worth, either. Let those extra few pounds linger if it means you get to participate actively and happily in life.

Not giving in to the temptation of a quick fix often takes just as much, if not more, effort than going for it. Seeing Jessica,

Jimmy, and Jane all lose 10 pounds in a week can be enough to send even the strongest of us straight into the arms of discontent. But I urge you, I urge us, to stop looking outward for our worth and instead, dig a little deeper inside. Let's have enough faith in ourselves to go against the grain to choose to love ourselves exactly where we are at, first and foremost. Say yes to salad, yes to cake, yes to balance, yes to joy, yes to taco Tuesdays, yes to wine nights, yes to sex with the lights on, yes to smoothies that make us feel like a goddess, yes to rest, yes to exercise, yes to being on top, yes to the things that breathe life into us and call us home to our true worth!

Your bikini body already exists, but tomorrow doesn't. The vessel your soul resides in wants you to live your best life, however long or short it may be. So throw it a bone and maybe a cheeseburger too, if that's what it wants. We can do hard things, friends. Even if those hard things involve letting go of the expectation that a "worthy body" should be hard to achieve.

May we never go hungry in the name of beauty again.

INTIMACY: CHATEAU DE FRANKLIN

"Intimacy is the capacity to be rather weird with someone and finding that that's ok with them."

— ALAIN DE BOTTON

ON JUNE 26, 2013, AT APPROXIMATELY 8:00 P.M., MY HUSBAND watched me defecate as I attempted to push our son out of my vagina. My knees were hugging the opposite sides of my chest, and I was bearing down during a contraction, trying to make this whole birthing thing happen, but last night's dinner came out instead. I pooped right there on the hospital bed, and I knew it, even though I couldn't feel anything other than extreme pressure and nobody spoke a word of it. My midwife swiped a towel to my body before swiftly tossing it behind her, like one of those women you see flying their bandanas up in the air to signal the start of a street race. Derek's eyes caught mine with the sort of shock and disbelief that could only come from watching poop pop out of your wife's body from a very intimate angle. *And he thought Human Centipede was disturbing!*

We took a prenatal course through our hospital where they

told us all about emergency C-sections, the risks of epidural, and the ring of fire. This is also known as the moment you realize your vagina is actually the gatekeeper to hell. That an angel is about to escape from Satan's grasp by turning your once firm hole into an inflamed circus ring, just so some magician, priest hybrid known as "Dr. Such and Such" can pull a human being out of your hoo-haw. Doc then immediately performs an exorcism to remove the placenta. You formerly thought it was your friend before, but it's now threatening your life with each moment it stays crammed inside of you.

They prepared us for swaddling and diaper changing and used a doll to show me the proper way to hold my baby to my breast. They warned about malnutrition, breastfeeding complication, and what to do if our baby was born with an extra foot. And at the end, they sent us home with an autographed piece of paper declaring Derek and me as certified to become new parents. But nobody, nobody told me that I might poop in the labor and delivery room in front of a nurse, a midwife, and my husband.

How could he ever look at me the same way? I just shit in front of him. Derek was an anxious father-to-be and actually scrubbed in to help deliver our son, but instead of bright baby blues staring back at him, he was greeted by a turd that I cannot describe to you *because everyone tried to hide it from me.* When I talk about this day in my own head, I refer to it as Turdgate. Sure, my son was born one hour and eleven minutes later. That was cool, and all, but Turdgate had burned itself into my mind, making June 26 a day of great joy and utter embarrassment for me. Months later, Derek confirmed my suspicions and understood immediately from my expression that we were making a silent pact never to speak of it again.

Learning to be sexy again after shitting in front of your

husband isn't for the faint of heart. I could handle the giant pads, the mesh underwear, and the stitches that stabbed my vagina when I walked, causing me to move around like a crab to avoid the pain. I could tolerate the swollen nipples and the mastitis and the sudden lack of basic human hygiene from sheer exhaustion and absence of brainpower to remember that showering is essential. Yes, these things could be dealt with, and I could do something about these things. However, I could never, ever, take back Turdgate. Thankfully, our brains can be our fiercest protectors if we let them. Mine put in plenty of overtime trying to wipe my memories clean as swiftly as the midwife had swiped the turd that shall not be named. Eventually, I was able to move forward from the horror that was my public defecation. I stopped fearing that shit would randomly leave my body every-time my husband tried to be intimate with me. But that didn't free me from a new set of challenges. Turdgate was behind us, but we had a new obstacle to face: an actual, human baby.

Babies are wonderful. They have this addicting smell that permanently attaches your nose to their skin and leaves you in a euphoric state of bliss that makes you feel high. *Like, one too many bites of an edible, high.* They're also a lot of work and my firstborn, Declan, is a rare breed of human. Moments after he left my body, he was trying to hold his head up as if he'd heard a rumor they'd be giving out medals for "Strongest Baby" in the nursery. The hospital staff were stunned by how strong he was. A month into life outside the womb, he was trying to stand and walk. There was no stopping him. There's still no stopping him. Declan never wanted to miss out on things, so he only slept in thirty to forty-five minutes intervals during the day. At night, he'd feed, rest for about an hour, then wake up to feed again. I could only put him down if he fell asleep on me first, and I transferred him. Even then, there was a 50/50 chance he might wake up the moment my warm body left his. Crib sleeping just wasn't an option. I honestly didn't press the issue because I had this crippling fear that if I left him all alone in the room down the hall, he'd stop breathing in his sleep. So instead, I slept on my back, and he fell asleep every single night directly on my chest where he could feel my warmth, and I could feel his breath.

He didn't like to be swaddled, but he also didn't want to be put down, which meant I spent approximately 20-22 hours a day holding him, rocking him, cradling him, and cuddling him. You can imagine how difficult it was to be intimate with my husband when we were working with very short pockets of alone time. Every once and awhile we'd trick him into his rocker or I'd be able to gently lay him down on the bed in a spot Derek had warmed up for him while I fed him to sleep. Then, if Derek and I wanted to be intimate, we got creative.

We're all adults here: we know there isn't a stork in a UPS hat that drops off little pre-diapered babies at our doorsteps, right? So it should come as no surprise that my husband and I created Declan the old fashion way. Meaning sex. We had sex. But just like those frisky dolphin cousins of ours, we like to have said relations recreationally as well. I know that people say it goes out the window once you have kids, but in our case that just isn't true. Sex didn't leave; it adapted. We knew we needed a new plan for intimacy. Our bed was off-limits because there was a baby in it, and standing up or bending over wasn't exactly the kind of mutually beneficial sex we were looking for. So one evening to make something happen, we grabbed a leopard print blanket and pillow and arranged them on the floor in front of our bed frame. This would be our new sexy space, and we'd call it, Chateau De Franklin.

Chateau De Franklin gave us a slice of intimacy in a room that had become more of a nursery than an adult space of two married people. There was nothing ideal about humping on the floor while our baby claimed the California King, but we were thankful for the opportunity to touch one another while laying down. It was around this same time that Derek realized our sex life was in a rut, but really, how could it not be? I'd pooped in front of him right before my vagina opened up the gates of hell. I recently retired a wardrobe of giant pads that covered from vagina to ass-crack under mesh underwear and my oversized tee shirts were always wet from my leaking, cracked nipples. Sex is part of my love language, so I genuinely wanted to engage in it, but I was feeling the emotional effects of being a new mom and adjusting to the changes in my body and daily routine. I knew he loved me at this point, but I was still subconsciously waiting for the shoe to drop, and this seemed like the perfect time.

Hell hath no fury like new motherhood. When you become the proud new, lifetime sponsor of a human being who cannot do a single thing for his or her self, it can have a severe impact on your confidence and mental health. For one thing, babies cry, and sometimes you can't figure out why no matter how hard you try, and that's a total mind fuck. It makes you question everything you thought you knew. Suddenly you feel like this utterly inept person. You wonder how none of the licensed professionals who walked into your hospital room flagged you as an unfit mother and stopped you from leaving with that baby. When I was wheeled down to our car with my fresh newborn in tow, I realized I didn't even know how to install the car seat. We'd forgotten to take care of it ahead of time, and I thought, *"Are they seriously going to let me just drive off with this kid when I don't even know how to strap him in?"*

Additionally, motherhood is the ultimate identity theft if you're not careful. The pressure to live up to the impossible standards our world has set for moms these days leads many of us into dark trenches. We forget about the person we were outside of our children because we're so afraid of getting found out as the terrible mom most of us think we are. We're given a uniform of messy buns, yoga pants, and slogan tee shirts. We're presented with a creed: *Mom life is the best life.* We're offered an allotted time of thirty seconds to ourselves before appearing selfish. We're also fed a heaping pile of activities, crafts, and chores to do from tummy time, to homemade baby food, to milestone markers, to monthly growth progress photos of our kid dressed to the nines. All while we spill coffee on our wrinkled shirt behind the camera in our spouse's sweat pants and five-day-old ponytail that's starting to hurt the scalp. Failure to comply results in dishonor upon our family name, not to mention the looming fear someone may call child protective services on us because we forgot to use certified organic apples for our puree. The threshold is unrealistically high, leaving most of us feeling like the *Looney Tunes* going up against the Monsters in *Space Jam.* Where's Michael Jordan when you need him? How are any of us supposed to live up to these insane expectations and still be a whole person? How do we claim a persona outside of our children?

I certainly wasn't feeling sexy like a Rihanna song with tiger stripes on my belly, tea bags for eyelids, responsibilities like a CEO of a Fortune 500, and the style of little orphan Annie (pre-Daddy Warbucks,). In fact, all I could hear was Mickey and his friends going on and on about hotdogs, the soundtrack where a mother's soul goes to slowly die. Derek spent his days doing what he'd always done; working for eight hours a day with plenty of adult interaction among him and his coworkers. But I'd traded in adult time for a stage five clinger who hated naps and loved screaming like a pterodactyl. I talked to a baby dinosaur all day long while my husband got MSN updates about news, politics, and pop culture. By the time he got home, it was almost as if there was a language barrier between us. I'd allege things he didn't understand like, "Our child wants me dead" and he'd say things I didn't understand like, "Did you see the trailer for that new Leo movie, 'The Wolf of Wall Street?'" I think a part of him couldn't understand having a baby for me was like having a midlife crisis for a man. My entire world was flipped upside down. Even though I loved our son with every fiber of my being, I'd lost myself.

Confidence was something I always struggled with, but suddenly, I was one of two friends in our entire combined circles that had a child. While my one mom friend and I dreamed of park play dates with our sweet kids, her family moved to Wisconsin, so neither of us got the sort of companionship a mom vitally needs during those first years. In fact, only in the past four years have our other friends begun to start their families, which means I spent over two years doing it without anyone nearby to relate or vent to. It was lonely, and it did a number on my self-esteem. I decided to try some at-home workout videos to get back in shape, hoping that would boost my spirit and by Christmas, I was down all my baby weight plus an additional ten pounds. The thinner I got, the more obsessed I became with exercise and clean eating. I thought if I could look a certain way, confidence would suddenly exist inside of me, like how a rabbit appears in a magician's hat after he says the magic words. For a while, I really believed I'd found the secret formula. It made me feel incredible when I told people I was a mom, and they looked at me in disbelief. *"You look so good! You don't look like a mom at all!"* I see the insult in a statement like this now, but then I was fueled by comments like these. But while I was working hard not to "look like a mom," I was neglecting to nurture other areas in my life, like my marriage and our sex life.

Sex was always something that connected the two of us, but now it felt like we were doing it for the sake of trying to keep our pre-baby life alive, and it wasn't working. We'd have sex every single night, usually on our leopard print sheep's fur blanket on the floor, but it was lackluster. I could tell Derek was thinking about who the Steelers were playing that week while I was counting the calories I'd consumed that day in my head. Thankfully my husband isn't the sort of man to sit around and sulk about a problem, so he brought it up one evening and resolved that no sex would be better than meaningless sex. But since neither of us really liked either of those options, we reached for plan C.

Plan C was terrifying. Derek had done extensive research on new and exciting ways to help me achieve orgasms. He believed the fate of our sex life rested in my ability to find pleasure in it. He was convinced if he could get me excited about having sex again, then everything would change for us and he was right, of course, but I was nervous. The kicker was that for this new method to work, I'd not only have to trust him entirely, but I'd have to give myself over completely, too.

"I want to try something that I think you and I will both really enjoy, but I need you to be open-minded, and I need you to trust me. You need to be willing to give your whole self to me. Can you do that?"

I'm not going to go into detail about what he proposed because I need to keep at least some aspects of my life private, but if you google the female orgasm, you'll come up with a slew of inventive and admittedly, sometimes terrifying methods to choose from that may or may not leave your face numb in pleasure. For me, I wasn't going to be able to indulge in any experimentation unless I could learn to stop being so damn insecure about my body and new role as a mom. I hadn't realized it, but every time someone told me I looked good "for a mom," he or she was actually feeding the belief inside of me that said since I was a mom now, I had to change. I couldn't dress, or talk, or fuck in specific ways anymore in the same way Julia Roberts had to learn how to use the outside fork first for her salad at that fancy dinner meeting in *Pretty Woman*. Accepting Derek's proposal meant I'd need to face my fear of losing control, my shame monster, my trauma, my fear of rejection, and my insecurity all at once. It meant I'd need to lean into his call for intimacy. I'd have to pull the shields down and let him in, uninhibitedly.

"Do you trust me?"

Well, did I? If the man who watched me poop right there on that hospital bed wanted to now explore my body in ways he hadn't yet, who was I to argue? If your husband still wants to spend time in your nether regions after a Turdgate scandal, you count your blessings and fall into him. I felt like Jasmin taking Aladdin's hand before he helped her onto the magic carpet and showed her a whole new world. I never could've guessed that Derek felt like Aladdin at that moment too, posing as a confident, "I know what the hell I'm doing" husband who wasn't also scared and nervous and praying to God I'd accept him and love him and understand him and enjoy what he was about to try. And so in true Jasmine fashion, I cocked my head, squinted my eye curiously, and said yes by taking the hand of this street-rat turned prince and getting on for what would become the beginning of a whole new world. It also marked a whole new chapter of my marriage and a whole new meaning for my life. When I fell into Derek, I mean, really fell into him, I finally knew what it meant to be seen.

UNPACKING INTIMACY

It's been a long day. A stretched out week. A hectic month. A fucking travesty of a year. Girl, I know. I've been there. I'm still there. Life? She peddles on whether you're all the way on the bike or not. And sometimes, that means you find yourself with half of your body hanging off the side and dragging behind the wheels, bruising with each bump you hit on the way. When you spend your days as a human vending machine, or a one woman bodily fluid clean-up crew, or a mediator, or a 9 to 5-er, or one of the other millions of things women do on a day to day that exhaust the shit out of them, the last thing you think you want is to then have to put on your best show for your partner for a quick wham, bam, thank you ma'am. You're channeling your inner Cinderella all damn day and wondering when in the hell your knight in shiny armor is going to come and save your ass and get you some fancy glass slippers and a tiara.

If I had sleep, personal space, romantic gestures, and time to put something other than leftover chicken nuggets in my system, THEN I'd actually want to get my freak on!

But instead, your partner walks in equally exhausted, overwhelmed, and stressed because life doesn't slow down for them either and they've been dragging behind the bike all day, week, year, too. So how do two people that spend their days keeping the world within their walls turning find a way to reconnect? Talking about your feelings gets a solid nod, because communication is important, but the top answer is one that may not immediately sit well with you, so hang in there with me.

The best way to reconnect with your romantic partner, husband, wife, spouse, or whatever you like to call him or her is sex. *Bow chicka bow wow, baby.* Now, this may a stir up big emotions in you. You may immediately reject this as being horseshit and sternly remind yourself that I know nothing.

What? Like you went to school for this or something, Andi? Get outta here with your pressures for me to have sex. You don't know what true exhaustion looks like!

Gentle reader, let me first tell you that yes, I do. I've survived the newborn phase, the newborn with a toddler phase, the midnight E.R. trips, the sobbing in my pillow all night over the death of a loved one, the agonizing sleepless nights that follow the loss of a baby, the "my mom has cancer and I can't get off of google" all night, the catching child vomit in my hands, and the moving into a fixer-upper with two children in tow. Exhaustion is an old friend of mine and the past two nights I've slept so hard that Derek could have hosted a fight club in our bedroom and I wouldn't have moved a muscle. I know, truly know, how crippling the lack of sleep and stress and anxiety can be. And I also know, truly know, that connecting physically with your partner is one of the best ways to ward off all those evil spirits.

Being intimate isn't always easy. Becoming a mother and entering into a new phase of my marriage where sex was suddenly a footnote rather than a main event highlighted this truth. But as I pulled this one from the suitcase, I could see that even before kids I was struggling with the big song and dance number known as s.e.x. I thought I only had a problem with initiating sex, but as it turns out, I had an issue with intimacy itself. Turdgate and new motherhood gave me an excuse to feel self-conscious, but I'd always been marking the moves. I stressed about my facial expressions, my stomach when it curled. *Am I coming off as sexy or seizuring? Did that noise seriously just escape my mouth? I sound like an idiot. I probably look like one, too.*

The irony is, I was so afraid of being seen and yet, I desperately wanted Derek to see me in all other areas. I was essentially saying, *"Here's all of me, but don't look down. You can never look down!"* As if my vagina were a Venus flytrap and I was saving him or something. I wanted to connect with him fully and at the same time, I feared what that might mean. It was easier to blame outside forces than to admit I was scared.

You may notice that there are similar themes in this chapter and the earlier one on control, but that's because the two intertwine. Control was the outer layer of a thickly coated issue. Learning to release it was one aspect, but learning to lean into Derek was another. Trusting him with my body and mind, wholly, was an act of bravery. I was stepping out of the wings and taking the stage. I was owning my fears and making a conscious decision to choose my husband over my insecurities and to choose intimacy over simply having sex.

If you don't trust your partner with your body, then ask yourself why. Are you allowing your own insecurities to hinder your growth and connection? The paradox is that authentic human connection is found in vulnerability, yet vulnerability is the scariest part of human connection. Will I be too much? Will I love too hard? Will they understand my love, or will I come off in a way that appears too clingy, too sappy, too content? The more comfortable we get with someone, the harder it can be to get vulnerable with him or her, too. We feel like we already know our partner and their limits, so we never really challenge that. We expect people to accept our growth while also keeping others in a box we carved out for them years ago. There's a trickiness here. You see it, don't you? My marriage has been most successful in this area because Derek and I are both aware that we'll never be the exact same two people who fell in love over a decade ago. We know that like the ocean, humans are continually rising and falling, pushing and pulling, following the current and crashing waves upon the shore.

Had Derek never approached me with the idea to expand and grow together in the bedroom, we never would've set sail on this adventure that has not only brought me to an entirely new level of pleasure, sexually, but has also allowed us a more full and satisfying relationship as spouses, co-parents, and friends. When our bodies are in sync, our minds follow suit; and we can then tap into a deeper level of human connection that I firmly believe is reserved for life partners. I think it's something we're all meant to unlock, and I credit that as one of the reasons why marriage is considered holy in most religions. This connection of body, mind, and soul is no mistake: it's why we were designed: to love and give love, to connect, and feel connected.

GRIEF: DOWN ONE WOLF

"You care so much you feel as though you will
bleed to death with the pain of it."
— J.K. ROWLING, *HARRY POTTER AND THE ORDER OF THE PHOENIX*

I REALIZED I'D HIT ROCK BOTTOM AS I WAS SITTING ON MY parents' couch at 5:30 P.M. on a Friday night, watching cartoons with a baby in my lap, an Uncrustable in my left hand, and a beer in my right. Derek was having his annual Christmas poker night at our house, and I wasn't in the mood to entertain a bunch of drunk men while breastfeeding a five-month-old baby and tending to a toddler, so I gathered up the gang and declared we'd spend the evening at the comfort of my parents' home instead.

As I headed East on the freeway, I heard a quiet voice that seemed to be visiting me a lot recently:

What if I just veered a little more to the left of this carpool lane? Would I be able to angle it just right so that the kids still lived? Would my children, my husband, the world be better off without me?

When I got to my parent's house, they weren't home, and the silence was deafening. Let's be real, it wasn't actually silent because I had a two-year-old and a five-month-old baby with me, but the house itself felt cold and uninviting. The door didn't creak, the refrigerator didn't hum, it was as if I was stranded in a padded white room with two screaming children and no background noise to escape into. I felt lonely and homesick and terrified to be the only adult in the entire house. It's not that I didn't trust myself; it was just that I didn't know how much more my heart could take on its own. So I did what any normal woman on the verge of a mental breakdown would do:. I hopped back in the car with my kids and drove to Sonic for a fancy-ass milkshake.

It had rich, creamy peanut butter and crunchy Oreo bits. Fluffy whipped topping and a maraschino cherry on top smashed under a plastic lid in a Styrofoam cup. I dove into that milkshake like a pastor dives into scripture. In that magical moment, it was more divine than an Easter Sunday service. It brought me to the yard, and I looked over at the McDonald's across the street like, damn right, it's better than yours. My children may very well have been plotting to destroy the world in the backseat, but all I could hear was the slithering of that peanut butter Oreo cookie milkshake suctioning out of the straw and sliding down my throat. Postpartum depression frequently has this effect on a person, and I was buried in the trenches, despite never watching myself fall. All I knew for sure was I needed that milkshake like a death row inmate needs a Porterhouse steak.

I made my way back to my parents' home and found them present but exhausted. My dad Karl had already made his way upstairs to turn in for the night (before 6 P.M., because this is what old people do and apparently the future I have to look forward to) and my mom was fiddling around organizing stacks of mail on the kitchen counter. So I let Disney Junior babysit my two-year-old while I grabbed a grape jelly Uncrustable and a beer and sat down to breastfeed my baby with hopes of coaxing him to a milk-induced sleep coma. As I curled up on the worn brown recliner, I was overcome with a sense of longing and tears began trickling down my cheek. I grabbed my phone and wrote in the notes: *I realized I'd hit rock bottom as I was sitting on my parents' couch at 5:30 P.M. on a Friday night, watching cartoons with a baby in my lap, an Uncrustable in my left hand, and a beer in my right.*

There was nothing particularly horrendous about this moment. I wasn't suicidal, financially struggling, getting divorced, or any of those sorts of things you'd generally associate with someone hitting the bottom of his or her emotional barrel. There was a beautiful, perfect baby boy fast asleep on my lap and an adorable, curly-haired, blue-eyed boy sitting calmly on the couch across from me watching Mickey Mouse Clubhouse with wonder. I could've called out to my mom, and she would've dropped every-thing she was doing to sit and listen and cry with me. Instead, I let my tears fall in silence as yearning filled in my chest and suffocated my heart.

I ached for the woman I once was, so optimistic and full of life. I'd always relied on her to pull me out of times like this with her glass-half-full mindset, but she apparently booked a one-way ticket out of here, and I feared she may never return. I yearned for passion. It used to pour out of me like hot molten lava, devouring anything and everything in its path but now, the only time I ever felt any sort of enthusiasm was when I was mouth deep into a Sonic milkshake, a piece of cake, a bottle of wine, a trough of macaroni and cheese. I itched for inner peace, for contentment, for joy. But mostly, I craved my husband. I missed him with my whole being, not because he was playing poker at our home forty-five minutes away, but because he'd gone missing nine months before that night, on March 6, 2015, when his lifelong best friend and brother died suddenly, immediately, unimaginably, in a motorcycle accident.

Brian was the living embodiment of carpe diem. I'll never forget the first time Derek brought me over to Brian's for a get-to-gether. We showed up on time, which meant we were actually an hour early because my husband believes in punctuality, unlike most people who attend house parties. We were greeted at the door by a brindle pitbull named Aries, the sweet canine alpha of the home who loved a good scratch behind the ear. There wasn't a soul in sight, and Derek ushered me to make myself comfortable while he went room to room looking for Brian. I scanned the shabby couches and couldn't help but feel like they were an indication of how much traction and love this place housed. Surely this was the hub, the home base for all of their friends and family with couches so well broken in as these.

From outside, I heard a robust voice shout, *"Der, Der!"* and moments later, a stocky man in a crisp Redskins hat and a black Tapout tee came strutting in the room. The entire place lit up when Brian stepped through the door in the sort of way that Christmas joy fills the air when Santa shows up in a movie. His look suggested he wasn't one to be trifled with, but his gleaming eyes and full cheeks immediately made me feel like I was home. After introducing himself and pulling me in for a hug, Brian disappeared into his bedroom and came back out a moment later with some pot.

"You want to smoke, Andi?"

I'd smoked a few times before with friends but had yet to engage in it with Derek, but I felt safe and comfortable with Brian, so without hesitation, I grabbed the pipe and took a hit. It wasn't until after the smoke left my lungs that Brian declared, *"We need to make a Stater Brothers run, guys. Let's go!"*

Derek was the only one who hadn't just smoked, so we hopped in his truck and made our way down the street to do a beer run. By the time we parked, I was high. So freakin high. I wasn't a regular partaker, and marijuana always seemed to hit me harder than other people. It probably had to do with the fact that I used to starve myself back then to be skinny, but I digress. I was super high, and since I was in foreign territory, aka the supermarket in front of a bunch of strangers, I got quiet. I was like a twenty-one-year-old mime following two dudes around and using hand gestures to communicate. I trailed closely behind the two best friends as they caught up on life and howled over inside jokes: I was a silent, high observer to the undeniable bond they shared. After what felt like a full twenty-four hours in the beer aisle, we finally left the store, and Brian let out a full belly laugh that I'd later learn was his signature.

"Andi, are you okay? You haven't said a damn word!"

It was love at first high. Brian welcomed me into his world, and I quickly became family. Plus, once you were Brian's family, you claimed a spot in his wolf pack. He'd fiercely protect you, love you, support you, and tell you off if you needed to get pegged down a notch. I immediately understood why Derek would follow him into a coffin-filled dirt ditch without a second thought if Brian asked. He was captivating, warm, and honest, and man, he loved Derek fiercely. The two of them shared a rare kind of bond that could only be born out of two small children who relied on one another for comfort, friendship, and survival. Their connection to one another was irrevocable. They talked on the phone daily; and even as time would pass between seeing one another because of life and responsibilities, once they were in the same room again, it was as if they had never been apart. It was literally as if they were connected by some force, and people could feel it when they walked into a space together. Crowds would clear poetically when Derek showed up because they knew his path was straight to Brian and nobody dared stand in the way.

For the next six years, I'd show up to Brian's with Derek and team up with his wife Kira in boys vs. girls beer pong matches. We'd drink Tequila Rose shots and play poker until the sun came up. The music was loud, the house was always full of friends who had become family, and Brian stood at the center of it all filling the air with Christmas like magic and making everyone feel more at home than they sometimes felt in their own spaces. Of course, the older we all got, the more life began to shift, making our partying less and our responsibilities more. Still, no matter how much time passed between seeing each other, we always picked up right where we left off formerly. As for Derek and Brian, the two of them never missed a beat no matter how much physical space was between them. Every morning after Brian grabbed a hot coffee and egg McMuffin from McDonald's, he'd call Derek and they'd shoot the shit on the way into work. The only thing that could ever keep the two of them apart, it seemed, was death. But even death was no match for the two wolves.

The night Brian died, Derek and I went on a date to this delicious Italian restaurant in Fullerton called Roman Cucina. I was just shy of twenty weeks pregnant with our second son, so no wine for me, but we feasted on crispy bruschetta and the best Bolognese either of us has ever had to date. We laughed and marveled at one another: our eyes glistened in the dimly lit candlelight as our hands touched, intoxicated from love. We chatted about the following day and his plans to go get a tattoo consultation with Brian. They hadn't seen each other in a while and I knew how time evaporated when they were together, so I was encouraging him to stay as long as he pleased.

"Just be home by dinner. Spend the whole day together. It's been a while, and I know you love being with him and hanging out."

We boxed up the rest of the Bolognese and made our way home to our oldest son Declan, who was fast asleep on his aunty's lap when we walked through the door. I scooped up Declan and hugged my sister goodnight before leading her out and heading down the hallway toward the toddler bed we'd set up for little man on the side of our bed. Once he was settled in, I brushed my teeth and washed my face before crawling into bed with my husband. We made love and fell into slumber with happy bellies and full hearts after a much needed, perfect date night.

About two hours later, I felt a jolt that woke me in a startle. I'll never know why he answered that late-night call. Derek was a chronic "Let it go to voicemail if it's after 9 P.M." kind of guy. I'll never know why, but he picked up and heard his dad Dennis frantic on the other line.

I lifted my head from the pillow and saw Derek standing grimly over the bed.

"What? Who?"
"Brian. Son, Brian is dead."

I could hear the voice on the other line say the word "dead," but I'd no idea who they were talking about and in my sleepy state, I thought he was talking to Brian. I assumed someone older had passed like a grandparent or something. But Derek's face was ghostly.

"Who died, babe? What's going on?"

Derek stood like a petrified tree for a long pause before collapsing his body onto the bed. Then a tone so shrill and deep at the same time escaped from him as he wailed, "Brian. He's dead!"

The howling. Deep, harrowing howling. His body was practically convulsing as he cried a howl, unlike anything I've ever heard from a human being before.

Brian is dead.

I couldn't process this information. Brian was our pack leader, he was Derek's pack leader; he couldn't be dead. I immediately felt overcome with a primal need to somehow shield my husband from his searing pain. He'd never experienced a huge death in his life. All of his grandparents still live and breathe as I type this, and death wasn't something he was accustomed to encountering. Not like I was. I always knew his first big one would be hard, but I never could've expected that it would be the most significant person in his entire life. What kind of backward God did we have that would let Brian die the night before he was supposed to see Derek? He planned to ask him to be the Godfather of our unborn son. There was so much left to experience with him. To say to him.

Brian died immediately on impact. He was riding his Harley and made a right-hand turn on a red light, not realizing that a GMC Yukon was making a left from across the way at that exact moment. His body was thrown several feet away, and he laid in the road with a sheet over him for hours while the police investigated the scene and his wife Kira stood three feet away frozen in disbelief. They wouldn't let her see his body there because his chest was so caved in that they felt it would traumatize her. He was only twenty-nine years old.

The day Brian's soul went to Heaven, a piece of my husband's flew away with him. I felt it leave his body that night, as he curled up in the fetal position and howled. Derek got out of bed the next morning and hopped in the shower. About ten minutes later, I watched him pull some boxer briefs out of his drawer and comb through his closet for a button-up shirt. He remained silent as he laced one shoe after the other, then kissed me goodbye and left for a morning meeting as if nothing had happened. I always feared that when he experienced death, he'd shut me out, and admittedly, I began to panic. It was such a delicate time, and my heart was hurting, too. My heart ached both for myself, the loss of my dear friend, and for my husband who had just lost his brother. The day the wolf died, Derek disappeared into himself. We stopped living and started surviving.

Four months later as we drove to the hospital and I made noises so deep they're only found in exorcisms and active labor, we clutched hands and wept to "Flashlight" by Jesse J knowing that the day had come when Brian's godson would be born into a world without him in it. New life was supposed to heal us, but it didn't. Instead, we were crushed under the responsibility of caring for two small children. One had already felt so overwhelming and adding a second to the mix while mourning an unthinkable tragedy like Brian's death, was soul-crushing. It was also magical.

Bennett Lee-Brian somehow lived up to his namesake, without

any help from his blessed but closet depressed parents. He had a smile that took up his entire face, making it impossible not to grin along with him. His little thigh rolls were the ones I'd always dreamed up in my mind that my first son, who didn't reach the 5% until he was 2, never possessed. I wish I could've bottled up his goodness and drunk it like a poly potion, soaking up his joy and basking in the warmth of content. Instead, we survived. Derek would get home from work and head straight out to his garage where he'd fiddle with the shadowbox memorial he custom made in Brian's memory or rearrange his tools. I'd put cartoons on and pray to God that Declan wouldn't realize daddy was home, lest he threw a tantrum over not being able to play with Daddy.

We still smiled and kissed, and talked, and had sex every night as if life were beautiful. I'd even post gorgeous photos of my children on social media in perfect lighting with a sappy caption about how hashtag blessed I was. We were the damn American dream, but we desperately needed therapy, medication, and healing. The truth is that Derek and I were both slowly dying inside. We'd creep around one another as if all the flooring in our home was broken glass. We didn't mean to, but we'd both pulled away from one another as a survival tactic.

Shields up.
All the way up.

I chopped off all of my hair, which is probably the most significant S.O.S. of women everywhere. Then I dyed it purple. And when that high wore off, I dyed it pink. I began drinking coffee from 4:30 A.M. until 4:30 P.M. when I'd switch to Pinot Noir. I ate leftover chicken nuggets and an excessive amount of El Pollo Loco chicken avocado salads. *With a side of macaroni and cheese. And maybe a churro? Yes, add the churro.* I was frantically looking for something, anything, to fill the void in my soul, but nothing ever seemed to last. I couldn't admit to myself that my marriage was unraveling because we hadn't touched a single thread. It didn't make sense to me that we could be so in love and so distant from one another at the same time. We'd always dealt with tragedy together in the past, and it'd always brought us closer, stronger. But while Derek was trying to be strong for me and I was attempting to be brave for him, we forgot that there was an "us" to protect.

And as I sat there on my parent's couch at 5:30 P.M. on a Friday night, watching cartoons with a baby in my lap, an Uncrustable in my left hand, and a beer in my right, I realized that my heart was reaching for my marriage in desperation. We couldn't go on another minute like this, I felt it in the depth of my stomach, and I knew it wasn't just the milkshake rumbling around in there. Something had to change, and it had to start with me, right then and right there.

UNPACKING GRIEF

How do you convince a man to heal his heart? You *inception* his ass. Derek and I refer to "inceptioning" someone as planting ideas or thoughts into one's mind and convincing them it was theirs all along. You know, like the mega hit starring everyone's favorite bachelor, Leo. This concept of inception is particularly useful when you really want pizza, or you need your spouse to think he was the one to pick the movie that night.

If you've never seen the movie, *Inception,* here's the rundown. Leonardo DiCaprio plays a thief named Dominic Cobb who steals secrets from big important people using a dream-sharing technology called, you guessed it, Inception. He and his team get tasked to do the impossible and plant an idea into someone's mind using Inception, and his team faces many obstacles along the way as Cobb's deceased wife Mal (played by the ever stunning Marion Cottilard) keeps showing up in the dreams and trying to bring Cobb home to her. In the case of Derek, he was my Cobb, and Brian was his Mal. Everywhere Derek went, it seemed, Brian would follow. There's a reoccurring line in the movie where Mal whispers to Cobb:

"You're waiting for a train. A train that will take you far away. You know where you hope this train will take you, but you don't know for sure. Yet it doesn't matter, because we'll be together."

Derek was in the station, waiting. He had his bags packed and a single rider, a one-way ticket to who knows where. Grief has a way of entrancing a person. Death anchors us to the grave and whispers sweet nothings into our ears, often leaving those of us left behind wishing we could sleep forever alongside the ones we've lost. For the first time in Derek's life he was considering the idea that maybe life wasn't worth sticking around for if it meant he had to live without Brian; and though it would be another year before he admitted it to me, I knew at the time that I was losing the battle to keep my husband off the train. I needed to inception him before the train came. But how? No amount of conversation or motivational speaking or bargaining would keep him from boarding. His heartache was blinding him to the beauty around and only highlighting the emptiness. My attempts to pry his heart open and pluck out the dying pieces like a game of Operation only pushed him further away. I was

losing him to his grief, and I didn't know how to help him heal;
so instead, I did what I could to make everything else in his life
feel manageable, so he'd have fewer things to distract him from
mending his ruptured heart.

I stopped complaining every time I had a hard day with the
kids, which wasn't easy because I loved to bitch and moan about
how rough my day was with the kids. I started making shower
time and clothes other than yoga pants a priority, and some days
I wouldn't get ready for my day until right before he walked in
the door, but I did it. I smiled more. I'd almost forgotten that
a smile was once my face's default expression. I greeted him at
the door with a kiss rather than waiting for him to come to me. I
started cooking again. I even kept up with the housework, rather
than letting the laundry and toys pile high like Mt. Everest. And
most profoundly, I stopped relying on him to make every single
life decision for me from whether or not we needed a plumber
for a clog to what I should eat for lunch.

Surprisingly, as I worked overtime to fill the cracks in my
husband's heart, I was unknowingly filling the spaces in my own
as well. It had never occurred to me how deeply I relied on Derek
for everything in my life. I expected him to make me happy, work
full time, play with our kids, make decisions for me, and not only
man the fort, but captain my life as well. Oh, and I also wanted
to be romanced, and wooed, and aroused.

*I'll keep your children alive, put dinner on the table, and keep
your house partially clean 15% of the time, and you do everything
else, okay?*

His depression forced me to acknowledge my co-dependency
because, for the first time in our entire relationship, he didn't

have the emotional capacity to carry my purse full of pain. This didn't sit well with me at first. I mean, wasn't it his job to carry my purse? Isn't that what partners are for? Sex, purse carrying, and killing all the spiders forever and ever, amen. Honestly, I felt betrayed and left behind, as if I was at the station with him but in a completely different terminal waiting for an entirely different train. It felt like every time I found him and dropped my luggage down next to him, he'd excuse himself to the bathroom and never return. Then I'd go searching again and see him at a different terminal, and the cycle would continue. I was never one to enjoy being alone, and suddenly I was alone all of the time, even with my husband physically sitting right next to me. I was forced to become my own best friend because the one I'd been relying on for years was nowhere to be found.

Entering into a friendship with myself didn't materialize easily. I spent the majority of my life talking major crap about the girl in the mirror, and now I thought she'd magically want to be my friend? After all the bullying I'd done? *Come on now. Seriously, you tell me I'm ugly almost every day. I don't want to hang out with you any more than I have to.* Me and myself had little to no faith in one another. We were like long-lost sisters reuniting for the first time after years of separation, pain, and neglect. There was so much to say and even more to heal, but both of us were guarded and uncomfortable. We were ready to return to estrangement, only, we couldn't. We didn't have that luxury anymore. Nobody was there to fill the gap between us. We were living on a prayer, alone on an island, forced to work together to find a way back to civilization. A way back to life.

Our start was painfully awkward. A blind date of sorts. What's our favorite color? What do we want to eat right now? Where should we take the family this weekend? While Derek healed, I was becoming the woman I was always meant to be. I was blooming into a partner instead of a co-dependent wife and learning to let go of the idea that I could somehow fix or heal my husband with the flick of a wrist. I stopped putting the responsibility for his happiness on my shoulders and instead, did what I could to bring joy into my own world in hopes it would pour out in our home and flourish at his feet.

One morning I woke up and crept to the bathroom to get ready for my day like usual. But when I looked in the mirror, I was floored. I thought to myself, there's someone here under the thin layer of skin, and veins, and blood, and muscle, and cartilage. Like a butterfly's metamorphosis, she's stirring, she's awakening. I knew right then and there I could keep erasing myself, refusing to speak up or out about my wants and needs, or I could step into the woman I was and fill the space I occupied. I knew if I stayed small, if I continued to shrink myself, nobody wins. When you stay small in your marriage, nobody wins. This was my chance to expand. I was like one of those little dinosaur-shaped sponges, living my life on dry land. Nobody told me I'd grow if I soaked in a bit of water. I'd been living my entire life thinking I was always meant to be tiny in stature when actually, I'd been designed to be massive. It was there within me all along. I just needed to add water. I needed to absorb, rather than shrivel, soak instead of dry. I needed to grow. Grow into me. Into the woman, I was always meant to be.

Learning about myself was fascinating. It turned out I actually had a lot of good ideas all on my own. I discovered new restaurants and new menu items from older ones. Derek practically went into cardiac arrest one morning when I ordered the seasonal pancakes from our local diner instead of my usual egg white, spinach, feta, tomato omelet with homestyle potatoes and wheat toast. The heart attack may also have been from the heap of gravy on his biscuits, but I digress. I took our family on adventures without even consulting my husband sometimes. I'd pile everyone in the car and take off, without a word about where or what we were doing. Sometimes I wouldn't even decide myself until we were on the road. I kept up to date with what was going on in the world. That way I'd have more to talk to Derek about than Disney Jr. or which kid took the biggest poop that day. Suddenly, I had in-depth opinions on things like gun control, the dangers of social media, and which celebrities were offering a positive environment for our youths. I was becoming, in every sense of the word. And as each little pore filled up with the water and nourishment I was feeding it, I grew like a lotus emerging from murky river water to reveal her brilliantly unscathed petals.

I no longer needed my husband to solve all of the world's problems for me. I didn't need him to make the weekend plans or choose dinner or take out the trash. Once I grabbed my heavy purse off the floor where he'd dropped it and draped it over my own shoulder, I realized I was ready to love Derek not for holding my purse, but for being who he was, which is precisely the kind of love someone needs when going through something as life-altering as losing a best friend. Grief had sent a flood to wash us out, and now we were slowly blooming again. It was separately, at first. I used to think grief needed a soundboard to bounce off, but that isn't the case for everyone. Derek didn't need me to pry him open and force his feelings out: he needed me to be a complete person, so he could be a broken one for a while.

Slowly, he began to brighten. I'm sure he did plenty of internal work on his heart during this time, and I don't take credit for how he was able to finally learn to live with the death of his best friend. However, I did Inception his ass, so I get partial credit. Now that

I think about it, maybe he was the one doing the inceptioning all along? Perhaps his sorrow was a clever ploy to get me to stop acting like a selfish asshole all of the time?

On our wedding day, Brian stood up for his best man speech and told 120 of our friends and family gathered to celebrate our love about the time Derek got new skates when they were kids. Brian didn't have skates, so Derek offered to share. He gave Brian a single skate—one from the pair—that way, they could both skate, even if only one-footed. Brian shared this story to illustrate what a wonderful, kind, loving person is and the exact moment he was saying that to Derek, Derek was thinking to himself that he wasn't kind, or loving, or wonderful. He just never wanted to be without Brian. He couldn't imagine leaving him behind.

Brian's death has had a profound impact on our lives in this household. Brian took the skate to Heaven, and it'll always live there with him, which means a part of my husband will forever glide there beside him, too. But that piece was Brian's to begin with, and I think when we accept death as a part of someone's soul, then we more readily accept when a piece of that soul goes missing when someone is suddenly ripped away from us the way Brian was. Grief, both mine and Derek's, taught me that I was capable of stepping up as pack leader, too. The great news about rock bottom is there's only one way left to go, and thanks to Brian and his legacy, I know carpe diem is the only way to live.

ANGER: THE BULL AND THE LIONESS

"Bitterness is like cancer. It eats upon the host.
But anger is like fire. It burns it all clean."

– MAYA ANGELOU

"ARE YOU FUCKING KIDDING ME?"

I overheard Declan, now five years old, scolding his little brother for ruining his aircraft made of brightly colored blocks.

"Are you fucking kidding me, Bennett?!"

I didn't have to wonder where my sweet five-year-old got a foul sounding sentence like that from because I already knew it was from me. That night I crawled sheepishly into bed with a generous glass of wine to drown out the day. That season I was blocking out a lot of days with cheap bottles of wine.

"Declan said, 'Are you fucking kidding me' today to Bennett. I didn't even know what to do. What could I say when he learned

it from me? I've never been an angry person before, but I've had such a hard time controlling my emotions recently."

Derek gestured for me to lay in his lap, so I pulled my shirt over my head and balled it up to make a pillow on his knee. I presented my bare skin to his hands like a canvas to paint with his fingertips. He stroked my spine with his trimmed nails and let out a deep sigh:

"It's okay, mama. You've been through a lot recently. Nobody expects you to be normal or okay. You're doing the best you can, and the boys know how much you love them."

He was right: I'd been through a lot recently. Only a month had passed since I found one of my best friend's dead, after all. And whenever I was awake, I could still see her glossy wide eyes staring at me completely devoid of the life I saw inhabit them for fourteen years of spirited friendship and soulful sisterhood.

Kaiti was the bitmoji queen. I honestly had no idea what in the hell a bitmoji was until one day she was flooding my phone with this red-headed, fair-skinned avatar in glasses that was holding rainbows, eating pizza, riding unicorns, and peeking through windows saying, *"I see you!"* They were colorful, sassy, and hilarious, much like their human doppelganger, and even though I never really understood them, I loved how much she adored them.

Rape, of all things, brought us together. During my time with Dean, he introduced us, thinking my trauma may help her through her own. Kaiti was two years younger than I, and I was instantly drawn to her. I immediately inherited this deep need to protect her. Despite knowing how impossible it was, I tried.

She was my chosen sister, a statement she proudly told everyone. So much so, that it confused members of my own family at my wedding and made them wonder if there was a red-headed stepchild somewhere in the mix, they'd forgotten about somehow.

Kaiti wore colorful bows in her hair, had an affinity for anything with sparkles, and always kept a spare pair of socks in her purse. Her relationship with chicken was complicated, but her love for all things French wasn't. She drank tea, ate croissants, and loved a good wine night. She was cultured, and crass, bubbling, and complicated, and she'd absolutely no idea just how wonderfully beautiful and brilliant she was.

There was also darkness. A rumbling that stirred; tricking her into thinking there wasn't a place in this world for her bewitching radiance. She openly struggled with depression as well as chronic physical pain. She tried to jump in water more than once, but so many of us tethered her to the bridge. Her body never made it past the edge because we gently pulled her from the railing time and time again. We'd cry out to her, "You are here. You are safe. You are loved. Stay here with us. Stay here where it is warm, dry, and safe. Stay here with us, Kaiti."

The night after I found her lifeless, I lay in bed watching *Planet Earth*, trying to give my brain something, anything else to contemplate. The narrator was highlighting bulls in Africa, and they were all in a watering hole. Suddenly, a pack of lions appeared and began circling the bulls. They all started to panic and flee, but the lions stayed diligent. After all, they didn't need every bull: they only needed one. The lions worked together to distract a bull while a lioness pounced on his back. She sunk her teeth into his shoulder, and I gasped as I watched him struggle to get her off of him. The narrator chimed in with his British accent cautioning, *"He isn't done yet. But to win, the bull must shake off the lioness."* A bull was trying to fight a lion. The scene ended with the bull losing his fight and becoming a meal for the lioness and her pack. I changed the channel and spent the remainder of the evening wondering if Kaiti simply lost her battle to the lion that stalked her for so long.

I don't believe she killed herself, at least, not intentionally. Still, her poetic soul died on October 10, 2018: World Mental Health Day. Somehow she made a statement with her death without saying a single word to any one of us. When I found her, she was already gone. I knew it the moment I walked up on her truck and saw her mouth and eyes wide open, completely void of life. When I called 911, the dispatcher told me to pull her from the vehicle, lay her body on the cold asphalt, and compress on her chest until paramedics arrived. It took all my strength to lift her limp body from the seat, and I fell to my knees when she began to topple me over, refusing to let her body hit the ground and using mine as a soft barrier. Despite my CPR training, Kaiti was announced dead by paramedics ten minutes later. Months after, toxicology would tell us she'd already been gone for three hours when I found her. Yet as I sat on the curb across from her stiff body, now covered with a thin white sheet, I didn't know that.

I locked my knees with the palms of my hands to steady their convulsing. Through the cracks in my fingers and the lens of my tears, the sky revealed no hint of distress, with its stiff clouds, peaked like a frothy meringue, resting over shades of salt-wa-ter-taffy blue. I felt betrayed by its magnificent display in a time of unprecedented horror, but to look ahead was to gaze at a fourteen-year friendship under a thin white sheet, and I felt equally cheated by the anonymity. The only other place to look, it seemed, was down at the loosely rolled sleeves, now crawl-ing past my freckled forearms; At the knees of my inky black leggings, kissed in dirt. Her body had slumped across mine like an anchor hitting the bottom of the ocean, leaving hints of a turbulent seabed on my palpitating skin. Now, it rested in the street like the molted exoskeleton of a hermit crab—life hollowed out of a once vibrant shell.

Three hours later, I found myself sitting on a bench next to Derek outside of our son Declan's elementary school. I'd just experienced the most traumatic event of my life, but school still got out at 2:20 P.M., and somebody needed to be there to claim our child. Since I was in no state to be left alone, Derek and I went together heavily. I looked at my hands and noticed two popped blood vessels, the consequence of applying firm, constant pressure to a chest. As I gained a sense of my own physical existence and appearance for the first time, I looked up and noticed all the other ordinary people around us.

"I was holding my little sister's dead body a few hours ago, and nobody here would ever be able to tell," I muttered to Derek. *"I wonder what other heartaches and tragedies exist on this lawn, right now?*

He was right: I'd been through a lot recently. It was easy to dismiss my anger because anger was a perfectly acceptable response to what I experienced. People understand you losing control once and a while under challenging circumstances and finding a loved one dead indeed fell into that category. Oddly enough, it was her death that made me take a more in-depth look at my anger. The only way to survive death is to slow down; and when you stop moving, you're forced to spend more time with yourself. You begin to see things about yourself and other people you never saw before because you were flying so fast through your life.

Kaiti's death brought all of my biggest fears straight to the surface. Everything triggered post-traumatic episodes for me, from a creak in the floor to someone entering a room without me realizing it. I was terrified to be home alone, which wasn't a good look for a writer and stay-at-home mom. So I spent months wandering stores, sitting in my car in crowded parking lots, muttering grounding exercises my therapist gave me to try and keep myself in the present moment instead of back on that asphalt with her. I didn't want to be around people because it felt like they wanted me to be better than I was, and I couldn't fake anything anymore. Not a smile, not a laugh, not a damn thing. In a way, I reverted to a child-like state. It was as if my brain stopped filtering my social cues because it was working overtime just to keep my body from trembling. My face and body language expressed precisely what I was feeling at all times. It was there, in my inability to mask anything, when I met anger up close. She'd been circling, using her friends to distract me until she found an opening to strike. When she pounced, her teeth sunk right into me as if the impression of her jaw was already fossilized on my skin. Anger, the lioness. I couldn't shake her anymore. Then I realized, maybe I was never meant to wiggle myself from her grip. Perhaps anger was never really the predator here? Maybe she was bull, and I was the lioness all along.

I didn't have to wonder where Declan heard the phrase. I knew it was one of mine, something that often erupted from my lips long before I held Kaiti's body in my arms. The truth was, anytime my kids would kick, or scream, or hit I'd pompously blame Derek's genetic makeup. *They've got that Franklin temper!* Yet *"are you fucking kidding me?"* was the catchphrase my child had acquired from my mouth. I spent so much time pretending to be a mouse, I even convinced myself. But now that I couldn't hide, my anger was free to roam rampantly.

Was I born an angry person? Did I need counseling? Was I one glass of spilled milk away from becoming a complete psychopath? Was my anger dangerous? Was I capable of harming others? Could I be trusted to live with something we're told is so sinister?

It was hard to come to terms with the fact that I'd been under a spell most of my life, believing I could cast anger out and away like an evil spirit. I wanted to lean into the reason Derek handed me on a silver platter, but I couldn't shake the lioness. I couldn't hide from myself anymore even if I wanted to escape. Experiencing death up close locked that in. Instead, I'd no choice but to see exactly what was laid out in front of me and what I found was a lifetime of justifying.

There was always an excuse, some outside force for why I couldn't keep my shit together.

I didn't get enough sleep last night. I've been really stressed. The kids are going through another milestone, and it's a rough one! Not enough caffeine. Too much caffeine. I had a long day. Hard day. Emotional day. I'm on my period. Someone cut me off. Traffic. Did you hear the way they talked to me? I'm not usually this batshit crazy. Why am I acting this way? This isn't me.

But it was. It always had been. I felt it rumbling my entire life, a slow simmer under the earth's surface. It was growing like a heartbeat in a volcano, right before it spouts off and destroys the surrounding land. I simply couldn't see it until there was nowhere left for me to hide.

UNPACKING ANGER

I broke my brother's nose in middle school. I've gotten so used
to telling the story in a way that exonerates me, so it's almost
impossible to remember the truth. *Chris moved the pillow, so it
was his fault! Why would he move the pillow while I was punching
it?* I became super skilled at spinning the tale to mask my rage,
but here's the no-bullshit version. The version I've never allowed
my brother to claim until now.

Chris is only fifteen months younger than I. My mom always
said she raised us like twins because we were so close in age.
Since I now have children of my own only two years apart, I can
see what she meant. We were close, but we also fought a lot, the
way kids do. I frequently picked fights, partially because I was
tired of having a living shadow for any and everything that I did,
and partly because I loved the sound of my own voice. I don't
remember our exact age, but middle school sounds right. Chris
and I were fighting over which movie to watch. I wanted Bird on
a Wire, but he was fighting for Terminator, and I'd no intention of
letting him win. Verbal shots were fired and whatever he threw
my way sent a rush of blood to my face, and I immediately got
up off the floor to chase him. He ran to his room, and I hopped
on top of him and started wailing. He put a pillow over his head
to cover his face, so I began punching at it. I imagine it was hard
to breathe under that fluffy headrest, so he pulled his face out
for air, and my fist plowed straight into his nose.

The moment my knuckles made contact with his skin, I knew
I'd messed up, royally. It'd be weeks before the break was confirmed and years before he'd get it fixed, and I couldn't fess up
to the fact that I had every intention of hurting him that day. It
all got very "Eye of the Tiger" quickly, with me movie montaging

my way through the thrill of the fight. I hadn't intended to do the sort of damage I did, but I claimed for years that I didn't mean to harm and that's a lie. I meant to hurt him: I just didn't mean to break his nose.

I've spent a lot of time thinking about this because it's the first moment I can recall the veil lifting. Before I punched my brother in the nose, everything else was child's play. We fought in all the ways you expect brothers and sisters to fight. It was innocent, normal human reactions to situations. But as I moved into an older version of myself, I began to notice that nobody wanted to be around an angry girl. Anger was unbecoming. It was ugly, and I couldn't be those things. I couldn't be un-agreeable, unlovable. I wanted to be the kind of person other people needed so that I'd never be invisible again. As a result, I held everything in impeccably. I bottled up the unsettling, the frustrating, and the infuriating. Anything that might cause waves stayed locked away inside of me. That is, until it couldn't anymore. When I punched Chris in the nose, it was like the escalation of my anger had been pressurized for so long and someone came by and popped off the lid, sending the true me exploding everywhere.

Chris was the first victim of my suppressed anger, but he wouldn't be the last. Unpacked, I've found countless incidents where I've steamed up and poured over accidentally. You're probably thinking, *"Andi, you told us five chapters ago that you threw a softball at someone's face, and you didn't think you had rage issues?"* But I honestly always thought they were isolated incidents because someone had done something to me or hurt me in such an extreme way. I excused my anger as being circumstantial because that way, I could still be lovable, agreeable, and kind. I could still walk around like Snow White, singing to forest animals and being the fairest of them all. Because laid out, that's exactly what I wanted and the only obtacles standing between me and sainthood was anger. I saw it as a plague I needed to cut out of my skin.

I was knee-deep into writing this book when Kaiti died, and the topic of anger was nowhere on my radar. I think one of the most significant discoveries I've had since I began the journey of unpacking is how many stories got stuck inside of the bag, even after I dumped it all out in front of me. Like loose change still clinging to the lining of a zip pouch, I was still clutching to the tale that anger was a guest who occasionally dropped in to visit rather than a permanent resident within me. In a way, Kaiti gave me the gift of transparency and clarity. Learning to live without her required all my energy, so I didn't have any extra to put into keeping the facade alive. And once the lioness was unleashed, I became acutely aware that freedom was all she ever needed.

The truth is, anger belongs to all of us. Females grow up hearing people scold them for their anger. Passion is seen as a sign of instability in a woman, while a man's is admired as conviction. We tell little girls to watch their volume, their tone, their attitude. *That's not how young ladies act!* So most of us padlock anger. We do what we're told we have to do to receive love and favor over what feels natural. We smile, agree, and keep our mouths shut, denying a piece of who we are and abandoning ourselves until we spontaneously combust from the pressure. Make no mistake, you'll detonate. Any emotion forced into dormancy will eventually find its way into the spotlight, whether you want it to or not. And you'll keep blowing over and over again until you learn to choose yourself first. Until you realize anger was never meant to live inside of a cage.

As a society, we fear anger. It makes sense, to a degree, because we see it as the cause of our worst conflicts, wars, and deaths. But anger isn't the enemy here. It's the bull. In our quest for peace on earth, anger was portrayed as the bad guy, the villain. Tales of its fury were executed so well that people everywhere began believing the hype and spreading the rumors of its dangerous nature. Like telling a child a story about the monster under the bed to get him or her to sleep only to realize all the story did was invoke fear and keep the kid wide-eyed and scared shitless all night. Is the villain the imaginary bed monster or the adult who created it? We've come so far as people, finally noticing the negative patterns affiliated with shame and demonization. Yet, we still struggle to accept anger for its normal part of our humanity.

Think about it: If we never had anger, how would we know our limits? Our boundaries? When we feel angry, it's our mind's way of saying something isn't right. It's an offering from our brains to check in with ourselves and see the more profound feelings at play. *Why is this making me so upset? Is something else going on to trigger this response? Have I reached a place where I no longer feel safe, secure, or empowered?* Anger is what tips us off to injustices, both in our lives and in the world around us. It's the friend who isn't afraid to give you some tough love. The one who notices when your boss has been taking advantage of you. The one who throws a cold glass of water in your face when you've been complacent in a lousy situation for too long. We need our anger just as much as we need our joy; but since most of us were told that anger is wrong, we treat it like a fly buzzing around near our ear. Like a nuisance, we can swat away until it grows into something out of a cheesy 80's horror film and devours us.

When you banish a part of yourself, it's because you don't believe that part is worthy of the dreams you desire. You're hoping if you can shove it far enough down the bag, then it'll just dissolve over time, but all that does is leave you with one less piece. You can build a beautiful life for yourself and start care-fully arranging all the edges together, but without all the pieces, you'll never feel whole. You'll always be searching for more. I'm not saying to marinate in a thick layer of anger for the rest of your life. This isn't an excuse to walk around with guns blazing and a chip on your shoulder. Soaking in a casserole dish of fury isn't the answer. In fact, unchecked anger is just another way to hold ourselves back from love. I don't want you to be angry, but I do want you to be the whole damn pie. And the only way to do that is to allow yourself to process your emotions, all of them.

Living in duality is an expression of love. Allowing our griefs and joys, our trials and triumphs, our hurts and healings to coexist freely is an invitation to love all of ourselves, not just the parts we deem acceptable. It's like trying to play on a see-saw by yourself. You can't. You need weight equitably on both sides to lift from the ground and the balance of both anger and calm to keep moving forward prosperously. To keep yourself from neither exploding or staying unfazed by life forever. When anger shows up, don't exile her. Instead, ask her questions. Dig a little deeper to uncover her origin. Listen to what she's trying to tell you and let her speak.

To win, the bull must shake off the lioness. We have to climb off of anger's back and let it roar. We can't rock it, or cut it out of our skin, or ban it to the bottom of the bag, especially not if we want to experience love in its totality, not if we're going to truly and fully live.

GRUDGES: DON'T CUT YOUR OWN BANGS

"Not forgiving is like drinking rat poison
and then waiting for the rat to die."

— ANNE LAMOTT, *TRAVELING MERCIES: SOME THOUGHTS ON FAITH*

I DON'T KNOW ABOUT YOU, BUT I SORT OF ALWAYS TOOK THE Plymouth rock approach to life. Brimstone and hellfire damnation sounded like fitting punishments for any wrongdoer. Since my moral compass was crafted in the heavens, I felt fully qualified to make these judgments about a soul. Oh, how mighty I felt on my monstrous rock, hovering over all those who wronged me in my life.

Grudges are a lot like deciding to cut your own bangs. At first, you feel like a goddess among humankind, locked and loaded with a radical idea in your head and a jagged pair of kitchen scissors in your hands. That first cut mimics the feeling of relief and euphoria you get from an orgasm or a good sneeze. You pick up momentum as you snip, snip, snip away at the heavy locks in front of your face that have been weighing you down. You start to look a little like Cruella DeVille at the end of *101 Dalmatians*, with sheer mania in your eyes as you steer your scissors, usually reserved for opening up Otter-pops or packets of chicken breast, across your eye line. When it's time to step back and marvel at your skills, you ooze with satisfaction. It isn't until you've spent anywhere from one hour to one wash with the new look that you realize you've made a terrible mistake. Just hours ago, you felt overcome with satisfaction, but now your stomach hurts, and you're googling if you can get e-coli from the kitchen scissors you danced all over your forehead. You realize that, no, you don't actually look like that picture of Zoey Deschanel you taped on the mirror as your inspiration; in fact, you more closely resemble Johnny Depp in *Willy Wonka and the Chocolate Factory*.

This is where the real fun starts. You may be feeling the physical side effects of a horrendous haircut, but you'll be damned if anyone knows it. Now it's time to search the internet for quotes about being bold, brave, and beautiful. You'll spend hours screenshotting a wide variety of them and then it's selfie time. Girl, you've got those angles. Work those angles. Drop your chin down a little more. Look off into the distance with a face that screams, *"I've got big thoughts in this brain, but also, look how cute I am."* Now filter, filter, filter. Then hop on the internet and justify your self-butchered bangs to the world with some caption like, *"Beautiful is a feeling, not a look."* Post, refresh, and wait for the comments to flood in about your bravery while you go on an Amazon search for magic hair growth pills.

The grudge and the ill-cut bangs are one and the same. Both feel great at first. There's a rush, a high that comes over a person when he or she feels validated in one's emotions. But holding a grudge is a lot of upkeep, just like bangs, which is something nobody really tells you in either situation. You've got to lather, rinse, and repeat that moment to keep the burning fuel inside of you alive. It's exhausting. Exhilarating. Exponential. Bangs and unforgiveness take up residency straight across your face and become the focal point of your whole being. What I'm trying to say here is, don't cut bangs; or, uh, don't hold onto feelings that fill you with resentment.

I was once the reigning queen of Grudgeland. *All hail!* Hating people who hurt me was a full-time gig, and I took it seriously. Nuclear war, serious. With the amount of energy I expelled to keep people hung up on the line of shame, you'd think I was a Victoria Secret model with chiseled abs and 0% body fat. Refusing to forgive people was hard work, but I was just the girl for the job, double-crossers warned. This wasn't a problem in my mind, so I never bothered to challenge why I felt so entitled in my merciless pursuit of never letting anything slide. Fortunately, for my grudgy self, holding things against people was not only socially acceptable, but it was also praised. I learned early on that if I could make a case for my feelings, applause would follow, and I was addicted to the glory.

With my vengeful heart and a piece of paper, I could pen anyone or anything into the problem and martyr myself simultaneously. As a kid, I scribbled down words about my biological father that were always met with sympathy, encouragement, and at least one person who made sure I knew they thought I was "so strong and brave." I loved every second of it. I drank up the attention from my abandonment like an elixir, drunk off its power to victimize myself and evoke support. Time taught me I could paint my enemies in any light I chose, leaving them defenseless to my impactful way with words and an innocent-looking face. This served me for years, though I'd never admit it. When asked, I'd make a convincing argument regarding the biblical advice to guard my heart and my own need to rise above those awful people and events. Only, in truth, I was cloaked in their words and actions. I replayed my biological father's exit as if it were my favorite movie. I drenched myself in the memory of every hurt, bathing in each salty drip. This is where the bloodlust began. Staring out the kitchen window in the house at the top of the street, with the curtains peeled back, street lights on, and a cul-de-sac full of cars that were in for the night. Clutching a $25 Target gift certificate and trying not to blink as I waited for the date with my dad that would never come. At seven years of age, I died and was reborn as a young girl filled with hurt, anger, and a grudge that could light any match.

It never occurred to me the fire raging in my body was really a disease claiming residency on my heart and feasting on me from the inside out. As I grew, so did the flame, and it began to extend further than my father, and across any person I encountered who hurt me. I became a bit of a mean girl, though, nobody would know it because of my dimples, kind eyes, and reputation as the sweet, innocent one. I shudder to think of how I would've felt if other people held the sort of grudges against me that I did them. It was reckless and cruel, really. But I couldn't see it. I couldn't discern how it was affecting the people around me, and even more profound, how it was seeping into all areas of my life.

It turns out the way you specifically react, think, and feel about others and what they do or don't do to you is directly correlated to the way you react, think, and feel about yourself. We're all one big fancy-ass mirror reflecting and projecting ourselves. When you feel a pooling hatred for someone, it's often because he or she represents something within your own self that you have yet to deal with and confront. Maybe he or she reminds you of someone who hurt you, someone you hurt, or perhaps

one shines a light on a dark part of yourself you've been trying
to run away from? Whatever the case, it all comes back to you.
You must find out why this person or situation is such a trigger
for you. Only then, can you uncover the antidote. Self-love, ya'll.
It all comes back to self-love. And unbeknownst to me, I'd been
injecting poison into my heart for over twenty years. When you
think of it that way, it's a miracle it was still beating at all after
the self-destructive abuse.

In the spirit of transparency, I need to admit that I stumbled
upon an epiphany on accident. I wasn't looking to work on my
heart, and I'd never connected the dots between my resentment
toward others (specifically my father) and my inability to give
myself over to love, passion, sex, fulfillment, and ecstasy. What
happened can only be described as divine. A life saved through
death. Transformed. Reborn. Made, a-new.

In 2018, my grandpa Jim on my father's side died. After eighty-
five years on this earth, he decided it was time to go home and
passed peacefully in his sleep about a month after I visited him
one last time in Oregon to say goodbye. He didn't know he was
nearing death. Dementia didn't allow him to hold on to much.
And so, also, he had no idea when we sat in the conference room
of his retirement home that we were all there to hug him one
last time and send him off to Heaven. I found myself clammy
and irritable on the way to his funeral. I'd talked previously
with my aunt about whether or not my biological father Kevin
would be attending, and the verdict was still out. I felt like I was
a little kid all over again, anxiously peering into every vehicle
that pulled up to see if he was inside. This wouldn't be my first
encounter with him. Five years prior, my aunt threw a surprise
party for my grandpa's 80th. Kevin had been clean for over a year,
the most extended period he'd ever been able to stay away from

his addiction, so my aunt invited him to attend and notified us ahead of time that he'd be there. At the time, I was six months pregnant with my first son and absolutely terrified.

The hours leading up to the party were filled with a million different thoughts. I tried to map out each possible scenario in my head as if I actually thought I'd be able to prepare myself to face the boogeyman who haunted my dreams for eighteen years. Throughout that time, I'd accumulated a collection of letters, songs, and poems that I swore I'd give to him if I ever had the chance, hell-bent on showing him all of the pain he'd caused me. Most were at my parent's house still boxed in their garage somewhere, but I'd hoarded a handful at home, and Derek suggested I take them with me.

"It may be your only chance," he nudged.

I skimmed over each one as I neatly pressed them into a folder. They were raw and real and ruthless and heartbreaking.

Age 11: "This is your daughter, Andrea, in case you don't remember me. I'm eleven years old. I miss you and all, but I want you to know I think you're a jerk..."

Age 13: "You've missed out on so much. You probably don't even know that I'm an honor roll student or that my friends and I are forming a band and hope to become famous..."

Age 16: "I would write you a letter, but my mother told me not to talk to strangers..."

Age 19: "You plague me..."

When I stepped out of our truck outside of my grandpa's retirement home, I was bombarded with emotions. My breathing quickened, and I was dripping in tears and fear. Derek pulled me aside from my brother and his girlfriend and reassured, *"Come on, mama, pull yourself together. You're okay. It's going to be just fine. Be strong for your brother. I'm right here with you, don't worry."*

I composed myself and was relieved to see he wasn't there yet when we walked inside. We greeted everyone, and my aunt came over to us and asked us if we were ready.

"I'm not sure, I guess we'll find out."

Grandpa was brought in, and we were all instructed to yell "surprise!" at the 80-year-old man, but I froze because as he walked in, so did Kevin. My biological father. The man I hadn't seen for over eighteen years. He was wearing jeans, a hoodie, and a beanie, which angered me. I thought to myself, ""*Wow. This man is seeing his children for the first time in 18 years, and he didn't even bother to put on a semi-decent outfit."*

But really, what wouldn't have upset me at that monumental moment? I was scared shitless and looking for any emotion to cling to other than sorrow. I avoided eye contact like a kid who doesn't want to get called upon in class. Finally, he was within arm's reach of us and made a move to say hello. A handshake and a barely audible "hello" escaped from me.

He sat a table away from us, closest to me, and I could feel his eyes on us with every word we spoke. I felt my heart begin to soften as I thought of Kevin not as my bio-dad, but as a person. A person who lost everything. A man who has spent the more significant portion of his life battling demons, and failing. Suddenly I felt horrible for him. I couldn't imagine being in his shoes, sitting less than five feet away from his children and feeling that there was nothing he could say to make us accept him, forgive

him, or love him. He was like a child who's too short to reach
the cookie jar.

I went to the bathroom and made a decision that I'd initiate a
conversation of sorts. Something small, but a gesture of kindness.
When I came back, I turned in his direction and spoke:

"So you are planning on going back to school?"
"Yes, at the end of this month. How have you been? What's new
with you?"

Well, let's see, what have I been up to for the last 18 years? I
kid, I didn't say that. Instead, I replied that I'd been working and
that I was pregnant with a baby boy.

"I didn't know. Wow, a baby boy. Boys are easier than girls. You
were a big baby: 9lbs 13oz."

It took me by surprise when he recited my size. I awkwardly
made a joke about coming out with a full head of hair, he told
me he had the flu, and our conversation pretty much ended after
that. When we were leaving, I went for the handshake, but he
reached out for a hug. I'd like to tell you that we had a long
emotional embrace, but instead, I did the uncomfortable one-
armed hug, and it was one of the strangest moments of my life.
Derek asked me if I was going to give him the folder and I told
him I couldn't. It didn't feel right breaking an already broken
man. And at that moment I felt like I could burn them all and
never look back. I didn't, though. Instead, I tucked them away
in a box at home, and Kevin began reaching out here and there
through Facebook. I was cordial in the way one would be with
the receptionist at the doctor's office.

A little over a year later, my brother got married and invited Kevin to the wedding. This decision shocked me, but I supported my brother and chugged a Mike's Hard Lemonade outside of his dry ceremony before standing before all of his guests, and my father, as he took his love as his wife. At the reception, I allowed Kevin to meet my son, who was now a year old, and I posed for a photo with him and my brother. Kevin had just hit his two-year mark of sobriety, and I was proud of him. Still cautious of my heart, but softening more and more with each day. I even considered the possibility of inviting him to Thanksgiving dinner. Then everything fell apart. In September, his girlfriend reached out to let me know that he'd relapsed. She emphasized she was worried about him and wanted me to be aware in case he wound up dead. I was absolutely devastated. Then and there, I decided I was done with him for good. Fool me once, shame on you but fool me twice, you know the drill. Plymouth Rock.

Fortunately for me, my life never really included him anyway, so cutting him out was easy, not to mention he fell off the planet and went deep into his world again. I heard through the grape-vine that he found himself in jail again for possession, but I didn't care, or at least, I didn't think I did. I was married to the love of my life, with two little boys now who would never have to grow up abandoned, like I had been. On paper, my life was the same. Nothing changed in me, so I never considered that my lack of change was a problem. That is, until my grandpa's funeral three years later.

Kevin never showed. It was a small service for the retired Air Force, Willy Nelson loving man I called grandpa. A handful of us gathered underneath a green easy-up, and my aunt decided last minute to forgo the traditional service for a conversation instead. People shared stories of the man I barely knew, thanks to my exclusion from my father, and I cried, thinking of all the missed opportunities to really get to know him. I cried a little for Kevin, too. He didn't attend his mother's funeral when I was a sophomore in high school because he was in jail, and I couldn't believe he'd miss this one too, especially when he was living a free man. I suppose though, that even if he wasn't barred in a cell, he was still chained to his addiction, making him less free than I thought.

When talking with my cousin about it, I found out that the reason he missed was that he was currently living on a dirt road somewhere in the desert, not quite here or there. He was a scavenger of the dry land, with no means of transportation. I could barely process this news. My entire life, I've had an especially tender heart for the homeless, and there I heard that my own flesh and blood had no place to call his own. I went home that day, cracked wide open. Homeless. Homeless? What would I do if this were anyone but the man who had abandoned me? I already knew the answer. And this is when I stopped cutting my own bangs.

I had an epiphany that night. An "ah-ha!" so deep within my soul that I laughed. Was the answer really here all along? Could it really be this simple? My entire life, I believed I was unworthy of love. I convinced myself that if a father couldn't love his daughter enough to stay, then how would anyone else love her? How would she love herself knowing she was so unlovable? Up until this moment of laughter and disbelief, it never occurred to me that maybe, just maybe, love had been mine all along. It was mine. Mine to give, freely. To my father, to my husband, and mostly, to myself. The love I'd been looking for my entire life was lying dormant inside of me, waiting for her moment to rise.

I reached out to Kevin that night. I stumbled over my message to him, still getting my footing in this whole forgiveness thing, and he read my words but didn't respond. I can't say I blame him. What do you tell your child bluntly asking if you're homeless? I'm sure he didn't quite have the words and clearly, neither did I, yet. After a few days, I had another realization. Inward, I'd already made up my mind I'd forgive him, and I loved him, but outwardly I was gripping my walls for dear life. I realized if I was to truly move forward in love, then I needed to tell him that. I had to tell my biological father that I loved him. This realization was an invitation. Choosing to outwardly love this man who may never be able to love me back in the same capacity was an offer to myself. It was an open invitation to live in unconditional love. If I were going to accept, it would mean the shackles and stipulations were coming off, not just in how I loved my biological father, but in how I loved my husband, my children, my friends, total strangers, and yes, even myself.

There it was: This tattered, stained, crumpled up piece of paper. I pulled the edges apart to reveal its identity. The ultimate gift addressed to a seven-year-old little girl. Addressed to me. Only this time, it wasn't offering me a Polly Pocket, it was inviting me to the trip of a lifetime with an all-expense-paid one-way ticket to a life of freedom and true love. It offered to transport me to the deepest kind of love. The kind that holds no stipulations or laws or pre-requisites. All I had to do was RSVP. That night I made a bold decision: I sent Kevin another message, only this time, I wasn't trying to guard my heart. Instead, I typed these words:

I just wanted to let you know that I love you. And I'll probably tell you that every week from now on, whether you reply or not because I want you to know there's still someone living and breathing on this earth that loves and cares for you.

He didn't reply, but he didn't need to. I meant what I said. He didn't need to give me anything in return. There were no strings attached, no hidden agenda, no tricks. I just wanted him to know that I loved him and that I'd continue to love him no matter what. It was three weeks of "I love you" before he replied. From there, he'd periodically respond to my messages. Sometimes with a simple, "I love you too," and other times asking me small questions or replying to ones I asked. Eventually, Derek and I made the hour and a half trip out to the desert to drop off some supplies for him and his girlfriend. The directions were tricky, but Derek grew up around there and knew his way around the unbeaten paths.

"Make a left on a dirt road. Follow it for a quarter of a mile, and you'll see wood planks made into walls. That's my place."

Kevin and his new girlfriend had scavenged the desert valley for abandoned things and came upon a small trailer. They decided to collect wood and build a wall around it, claiming this piece of property and land as their own. Fortunately for them, the desert of Phelan is a wasteland and whoever owned this chunk of land wasn't coming to check on it frequently, if ever. So they'd settled in and made a charming little paradise for themselves within their wilderness walls.

I speak to Kevin weekly now. Our conversations, while still mostly surface, have found themselves more in-depth and more full of love in this year of weekly "I love you." I talked to him when I found Kaiti, and he came to me when the cold winter set in, and they had no source of heat out in the desert, completely exposed to the chill of the mountains and snow. I'm functioning well in our dysfunction, expecting nothing and giving because

I want to and for no other reason. It's an endless supply of pie here, you guys. Seeing it for all it is, every last slice, and knowing I sifted through the lies and heartache to hand roll the crust, the foundation. I did that. I made a conscious decision to climb down from my high and mighty rock on a hill and come face to face with my biggest offender. I looked him in the eyes, took his hands, and freed him from my expectations, anger, and hurt.

My entire life, I was looking for love in all the wrong places, when love was mine all along. Learning to love Kevin taught me how to love myself. Surely, if I could love the one who started it all, then I'd have to also love myself, the one who ended it.

UNPACKING GRUDGES

I spent 23 years on an empty battlefield with my ammo loaded, gun cocked, waiting patiently and obsessively for my enemy to arrive on the top of the ridge. Winter after winter came, still no foe insight. Bones chilled, fingers frozen to my weapon—standing my ground. Sure that when they arrived, I'd be ready to take the first shot. Then something miraculous happened. The 23rd spring came. As my icy fingertips thawed and the sun warmed my aching limbs, I noticed a tiny puddle at my feet. In it, I saw my reflection—this tattered, weathered, beaten down woman no longer looked like the girl I remembered. As I stared at her sharp browed eyes and passioned scowl, it all made sense. The enemy, it turns out, was me.

For who held me to that ground? Who left my body and mind for dead on a battlefield for 23 years? Who wasted energy standing and carrying a rifle filled with resentment through long winters and sweltering summers? Who cried out in angst?

Who watched the colors change on the leaves and counted down to a day of reckoning that would never come? It was me. It was always me. My revenge, my unforgiving heart, my constant desire to show my enemy just how badly they'd hurt me—it wasn't keeping them up at night. It wasn't holding them to a field, arms shaking and worn from the weight of their gun, their story, their anger, their pain. They weren't the ones weathering the battlefield. They may have spent their winters warm and inside. Cozied up, perhaps with a good book and a crackling fire? The only one hurting from my insufferable grudge was me.

Too often we look at our own lives as transformative, while looking at others as a lost cause. We act like we're the only ones that can go on the spiritual journey to grow or transform into a new person. We hold onto our grudges, clenched so tightly that we don't leave any space for people to grow within the walls we've created for them. So we still talk about people in present tense such as *"Oh, her? She's such a liar! Him? He's a Backstabber. Them? They're terrible human beings." He/she did these awful things, you don't want to know that person. I don't want to know that."*

I think we like to mask our unattended hurts with validation because deep down, we're afraid of what would happen if we let go. Where would our story go? How would people sympathize or side with us if we stopped holding on to the pain and allow our wrongdoers off the hook? It's a scary thought, a world without our stories. I mean, what if the person who hurt us changes in such a profound way that our story suddenly seems weightless? What if nobody believes or validates our pain anymore because it feels too farfetched? In this way, it feels like we've got no choice but to keep a firm grip on the narrative. After all, we can't let them get away with what they've done to us, right?

Or maybe the real issue lies even deeper under the surface. Perhaps we can't let them out of the character we've created for them because then we'd have to release ourselves from of our own. Then we'd have to lean into hard truths about ourselves, we'd have to look inward instead of out for the answers to our discontentment. When I forced myself to get uncomfortable and ask the hard questions, I found parallels between Kevin and me that were really hard to process. The biggest was that I allowed my biological father's addiction to turn me into an addict as well. My drug, however, was my grudge. Without hate fire in my heart to keep me safe, where would I land? In the arms of a rapist? A cheater? A betrayer? Well, all of those things happened with my hate, entirely intact, so how could I claim it was somehow protecting me from getting hurt? I couldn't.

All my grudge was doing was anchoring me to a story my soul was trying to outgrow. The lie I clung to was that I wasn't enough for my father, but the truth was it was never about me, to begin with. I was trying to compete with a chemical compound in his brain that was addicted to methamphetamine, and the more I sat on it, the more I realized that his addiction was only worse than mine because he couldn't mask his like I could. When you're drunk or on drugs, the outward effects are evident, but when you're power-drunk on revenge and high on hatred, you can still slap a smile on your face and throw your Jesus hands in the air without anyone blinking an eye in your direction. I was trying to filter my way through a lifetime of homemade bang cuts.

Reinhold Niebuhr advised, *"Forgiveness is the final form of love [1],"* and I finally know what he meant. You cannot love yourself fully until you accept that nobody is exempt from hurting us or being hurt by us. This isn't a get out of jail free card for the offender. I'm not saying that you should just let people walk all over you and say, *"it's cool, I forgive you!"* as they continue to commit crimes against you. Boundaries are beautiful tools of self-respect, and you have every right to decide that some-one need not be invited to Thanksgiving dinner or even to your friend's list on social media. What I'm suggesting, however, is that when you choose to forgive someone, you're also offering yourself a wonderful gift. You're gently expressing, *Self, I love you enough to free you from this hurt. You don't need to be bound to the pain this person has brought forth. You don't have to stay on that rock. It's cold and windy up there, and you could really use a blanket and a cup of tea by the fire. Come down and let me take you to the path of healing and love.*

Friends, do you want to know a secret? Nobody is thinking about you as much as you think someone is, and the reason is simple. People are thinking mostly about themselves, just like you are. When you dwell on a grudge, you aren't dwelling on the person who wronged you; instead, you're solely thinking about yourself. You feel hurt, you are angry, you want an apology, you, you, you. Why, then, does it become someone else's responsibility to fulfill your needs? The truth is that nobody will take care of you, but you. I know that sounds harsh, but it's liberating.

Imagine if we honestly had to rely on other people for our own happiness and contentment. That would mean we held equal responsibility for other people's joy and satisfaction. I don't know about you, but that feels like a tall order that I'm glad I don't have to fill. It can be hard enough to fulfill my own needs, and I'm me. I cannot even begin to imagine what it'd look like if I had to play the guessing game with others' emotional needs, too.

The most significant part of this whole I'm-the-boss-of-me thing is that you get to decide how you want to live. You're in the driver seat here, nobody else. So, why let yourself live in a way that doesn't bring you joy? Why hold on to expectations when you can create a life of abundance? If you take anything from my experience, I hope it's this: Forgiveness is the most remarkable, already-built-inside-of-you gift you can give yourself. It already exists. You just have to reach in and pull it out like a rabbit in a magician's hat.

My twenty-three-year stint on the battlefield was an elaborate mission for a grand gesture from my biological father that he'll never be able to grant me. Learning that forgiveness was never his to earn but rather, mine to give, has profoundly changed me. I'm finally free. Free from expectation, from the pain of my past. From the weight of my rifle and stiff body on an empty field. Free to forgive, to love, to live.

I won't lie to you and say it's easy, at least not at first. I was a bit like a child learning to read for a while. I fumbled when I spoke and had a hard time articulating what I was trying to say. When you forgive without the socially expected apology first, there's a big ass learning curve. Most of us have grown up hearing that people need to earn our love, and that can be a difficult reality to unlearn. However, I promise the work is worth the liberating result.

One spring day, you'll step outside from the warmth of your home and see a puddle from the thawed out snow. You'll gaze in its ripples and spot your reflection—this bright-eyed, wide-smiling woman—and you'll be filled with joy as you whisper, *"It was me. It was always me."*

SELF-WORTH: A ONE WAY TICKET TO PLEASURE ISLAND

Every woman that finally figured out her worth, has picked up her suitcases of pride and boarded a flight to freedom, which landed in the valley of change."

— SHANNON L. ALDER

"YOU NEVER INITIATE SEX."

The time had come for me to rewrite this truth. It was Derek's birthday, and he had a bold request: a day dedicated to sex. He wanted our bodies to enter a marathon dance competition with one another, and he wanted me to plan it all. This was my chance: My big break! My opportunity to seize the spotlight and show Derek that I wasn't some insecure meek girl, I was a woman. I could be an opener, an instigator, a let's-start-this-day-off right-er. I could command the space I was in, give myself over to pleasure, and take charge of both our desires. I could initiate sex.

I took his birthday request seriously and decided we should spend the weekend at his family house on Catalina Island. It was important for the plan that we didn't end up somewhere we've never been because both of us are explorers; and I knew if we chose a new destination, then our desire to see the sights and find a back-alley hole in the wall restaurant would overshadow our weekend sexcapade. Since I never do anything half-assed, I planned outfits and characters and even made him a brochure I cleverly labeled "Pleasure Island" that gave brief descriptions of the amenities of this "sex hotel" he had entered and the characters/activities to expect. I devised a menu of sorts, if you will. I reasoned that if I committed on paper to each role, then I'd stay motivated to follow through completely.

We boarded the Catalina Express that beautiful April afternoon and made our way to the captain's quarters with our free drink vouchers in tow. Derek and I both ordered some Pinot Noir, and the boat rocked gently with the waves as I opened up my laptop and began writing the first chapter of this book. It seems almost kismet that this book would end where I started it, middle-rowed on a charter boat sipping wine with my husband and preparing myself to make good on a promise I'd made to uncover why I was so afraid of initiating sex and then, to conquer it. I didn't know it then, but my journey of self-discovery was far from over. I was just starting to skim the surface of what would become the most important mission of my life. This voyage to self-worth, self-love, and self-acceptance was only beginning to set sail. I was about to embark on the adventure of a lifetime.

A quick cab ride through Avalon led us up to the Easter green, three leveled house overlooking the Pacific Ocean that Derek's great grandparents once lived in as residents of the island. We hadn't made a trip to Catalina in almost five years, but everything felt familiar and comforting inside those walls littered with memorabilia and love. It was a safe place, somewhere I could be myself and let my guard down freely. It was our home away from home, even after being gone for so long. We descended down the steep stairs to the second level of the house, passing the motorized stairlift chair his grandparents had installed for his great grandparents to get around easier and made our way to the retreat room of the house. The room had a half wall, like a pass window and to the left was a king-size bed resting upon a grand headboard. To the right, there was a living space with an old polyester couch, television, and impressive custom wet bar with thousands of dollars' worth of high-quality alcohol that had probably been there for over ten years. As Derek walked around the room reminiscing and gliding his fingertips over the craftsmanship of his late great grandfather's bar, I snuck my homemade brochure on the pillow and waited anxiously for him to take notice.

"Oh, how sweet! Grammy must have made this for us. What the fuck? Pleasure Island?"

Yes, babe, your 73-year-old grandmother made a brochure titled "Pleasure Island" with activities like "French maid" and "Nurse Andi" as your tour itinerary. She and I are very close that way.

Once he got over the trauma of thinking his sweet grammy had created a sex brochure, he was eager with anticipation, and there were no take-backs. Derek's birthday sex weekend was underway, and it was time for me to strap on my big girl panties, or rather, pull out my first outfit, and show the man I loved I wanted him just as much as he desired me. I was like the Little Engine That Could, pumping myself up and repeating, "I think I can I think I can" as I slipped into the bathroom and got ready for the first excursion on the brochure. I'll spare you the details for my husband's sake, but first up was the French maid and well, there was a lot for me to clean, if you get my drift. *Wink, mother fucking, wink.* I was feeling full-blown goddess after a successful round of initiating and taking control, and we decided to go into town for some lunch and drinks before returning for the "nurse check-up."

In Avalon most of the homes were built in conjunction with the mountains, so most people travel by golf cart to get around the island. So we hopped in the custom cart his grandpa designed to look like a model A Ford and made our way to the Cantina. Anywhere with Derek is my favorite place. We love each other fiercely, but we also really like one another. The conversation and laughter were flowing right along with the margaritas and tortilla chips. We giggled like two school crushes passing notes in class, sneaking quiet quips about what had just transpired behind the waiters back so as not to reveal ourselves. After lunch, we carted our way back up the curves of the mountain to the house, and I excused myself downstairs to get into character and ready for the next show. As I pulled the racy red and white outfit over my body, it registered that perhaps Mexican food and margaritas weren't the best choice for a woman who was about to put on lingerie in the daytime and act as a nurse sexually examining her patient, but I remembered the challenge I'd been given and rallied myself into character.

I rolled my shoulders back and walked out of the bathroom, a little self-conscious, but ready to show Derek I could do it. I could have sex with natural light in the room. I could be sexy and in charge and all of the things. I could initiate sex. Then, shit hit the fan. Or, rather, Derek slowly descended down the stairs in his great-grandpa's motorized stair lift chair. I should've found the moment hilarious, but instead, I was furious. *Doesn't he understand how hard it is to get into character? I spent the last 20 minutes talking myself up in the bathroom, and I walk out to jokes? This guy has jokes?* It felt unreasonable to be as upset as I was, but I couldn't stop the blood from rushing to my face and feeling embarrassment kick up the old "you're not good enough" dust. There I was at the bottom of the stairs in a nurse outfit that now felt ridiculous and unflattering, and I couldn't shake the flood of self-doubt pooling up inside of me. At that point, all chances of rallying and getting back into character were squashed. Nurse Andi met her slow death at the wheels of an old stairlift, may she rest in peace.

SHIELDS UP.

How did I get here? Was I really going to ruin this entire day I'd been planning for weeks over a poorly timed joke? I could have. It wouldn't be the first time. I saw my walls rapidly forming around me, closing in and cocooning me. Those shields had kept me safe, right? Or were they really just keeping me from my life? It was time to make a choice. I could continue to hide from the sun, afraid of its burn, or I could step out bravely into its light and take my chances with its rays. If I loved Derek, sex, and myself the way I was claiming to, then it was time to let my guard down and allow myself to be vulnerable, soft, and human with him.

SHIELDS DOWN.

I crawled over to my confused husband and kissed him with passion. I let the kiss release all of my self-consciousness, all of my fear, all of my shields. I caressed his body and dug my claws into his skin and refused to let go. I was officially in the ring. All the way in and ready to show up wholly myself. Nurse Andi may have died a slow motorized death, but I didn't need her anymore. I didn't need to step on stage and play a role to initiate intimacy. All I needed was the courage to put myself out there and then trust that when I did, Derek wouldn't only accept me but fully embrace me with open arms. I was no longer a resourceful mother fucker, a cool chick, a master of manipulation, or a closet sexual being ashamed of her desires. Finally, I was me, and I was ready to let all of me escape the prison I'd built for the bits that scared me.

SHIELDS SHATTERED.

We finished the evening with a beautiful sunset dinner, some embarrassing karaoke with the locals, and my final character; A new one that Derek and I both had yet to ever see. A woman fully stepped into herself. One who knew what she wanted, when she wanted it and wasn't afraid to command her space. The woman who had been stirring was finally awake. I called her, Miss A, but really her name is mine. Miss A is the side of me who had been dormant my entire life, and I was finally ready to set her free.

UNPACKING SELF-WORTH

I won't pretend a weekend sexcapade magically cured me of a lifetime of insecurity and a lack of self-worth. I still fight the urges to build walls around myself. But now that I know the love I always wanted is securely inside of me, I no longer put that weight on other people's shoulders. Miraculously, taking full responsibility for my feelings, thoughts, and desires has tapped into the purest form of myself. I was once so hyper-focused on everyone who didn't love me rather than noticing everyone who did. Rather than seeing my own soul crying out to me, shouting, *"I'm here! And I love you more than any other person ever will. Let me out. Let me free. Let me free you from your shackles!"*

In essence, I really had been looking for love in all the wrong places all along. I even tried to find it within my husband, which is what we're all taught to do. But that lead me down a path of co-dependency rather than partnership. It was only by unpacking my entire suitcase worth of lifelong baggage collected from my trials and triumphs that I was able to see the bigger picture. When we refuse to confront our issues they don't magically disappear, they just get shoved down into our bag and continue to show up in different situations and circumstances until we unpack them. All the stories I've shared in this book are connected by a lack of self-love. The absence of love for myself was present in every abandonment, shame, trauma, rejection, betrayal, comparison, grief, control, insecurity, and grudge in my life. I read a quote recently by Nayyirah Waheed that proclaimed, *"You don't have to learn how to love yourself, you just have to remember there was nothing wrong with you, to begin with. You just have to come home."* [1] All my life, I'd been waiting to come home and finally, I've arrived!

Now I know who I am. I always have, I think I just couldn't accept her. But it's a revolutionary feeling to know who you truly are. It's empowering to see your ugly bits as clearly as your beautiful ones and still feel worthy. Today, I embrace my body, soul, and mind with open arms. I've learned to stop putting conditions on the love I have for myself, and it has led me to a level of joy, peace, and pleasure I never imagined existed.

I never felt good enough for love before, but now I know I'm more than that. I'm entitled to the love within me. And when you tap into that kind of deep love, it flows out of you like a geyser. And when love gushes out of you so abundantly, there's literally no space for anything else. Love flushes out the hate, the suppressed anger, the grudge. It pours over everything and leaves you feeling fulfilled from its power. Learning to love the dusty forgotten pieces of myself along with the shiny and new has broadened my perspective of others as well. It has helped me tap into the truth that if I can grow and change, so can they. If you believe you can change, if you think you've transformed in your life, then you must also extend that belief to others. Don't hold people in a box while allowing yourself to expand but also, never expect them to become people they aren't. Choose to either accept them as an evolutionary being like yourself or move your story forward without them and wish them well on their own journey of self-discovery. This is an act of compassion toward others, but it's also a form of self-love.

There isn't a single person in this book that I don't wish well. Not a single one. If my rapist never raped another woman again and became someone of moral and kindness, I'd praise the heavens and throw a party in his honor. Seriously. I want all people to succeed in changing their lives just as I have. I don't want them to stay horrible so that I get to hate them for the rest of my life, because my life no longer has the vacancy for hostility. I hope that all of us become the very best versions of ourselves because the world needs people who aren't afraid of love.

I think it's important to mention that my adventure with unpacking is far from over and that's a good thing. While I've dug all the heaviest items from my bag, that doesn't mean more aren't sneakily tucked away in crevices or stuck to the walls with

LOVE, UNPACKED

old pieces of gum. Anyone who tries to tell you they've hit the
climax of personal growth and evolution is trying to sell a lie. In
truth, your higher self will always be a shelf taller than the day
before and that's the point. To keep reaching, keep learning, keep
growing and stretching your mind and soul. Maybe you'll level
up to the highest version of yourself for any given day, but of all
time? I don't know about you, but I sure hope I haven't already
peaked at 32 years old because then there's nowhere left to go
but down. A grounded plane is scrap metal, a grounded person
is complacent. And friends, we weren't designed to sit in a garage
and collect dust, we were created to soar.

In closing, your journey will look different than mine. Our
demons all wear different faces, but they're demons all the same.
If you only leave this book taking one thing away, let it be this:
You deserve the love you desire, and if you don't have it yet, it's
because you haven't looked inward. Inside of yourself awaits all
of the answers you seek. I can't tell you how to get there because
I haven't walked a mile in your shoes. I know life looks different
for all of us, and I'll never try and downplay the fact that despite
my many trials, I'm still a white middle-class woman in America;
thus, I was born into privileges that many of our population
don't have. Please don't misinterpret me: I'm not trying to fill
your bag with blame or convince you that all your problems are
fixable with some deep thought and meditation. Instead, what
I'm suggesting is that love is yours if you want it. It already exists
inside of you, and there isn't a person, circumstance, or natural
disaster that can rob you of that. It's yours because it comes
directly from you. It's braided into your DNA, woven into the
fibers that hold your body together. Somewhere along the line,
we just all lose sight of it. Life happens around us, to us, and our
love goes into hiding to try and protect these vessels of ours from

damage. Unfortunately, without the presence of our self-love, we grow susceptible to society's ideas and opinions.

Sex and intimacy become taboo. Shame festers like a boil. Other people's opinions of us become more important than our own. We stop being who we are and start molding into who we think we have to be for love, forgetting that love once roamed free through us before the world threatened to test it. Then we shoved it away secretly for safekeeping.

My story isn't particularly unique and that's why it needs to be told. Because so many, too many, people have downplayed their traumas because it didn't feel "big enough." But big enough for who? What shapes you shapes you. It doesn't matter how big or small the world views it. You don't have to live through front-page worthy drama to experience lifelong problems. Women are suffering in the shadows of their pasts without even realizing it. Maybe you're one of them, dear reader? Perhaps you don't know what it feels like to give yourself over to desire because you don't trust someone else with your body and soul or possibly you don't even trust yourself with your body or soul because you don't feel worthy. Because you don't feel validated complaining about your life when it all seems reasonable enough on paper even though you feel a void deep in your heart. Because you've got no idea that the love you've been searching for is inside of you already, just waiting for its chance in the sun.

Well, I'm here to tell you that your story matters and so do you. Your story is real, but the one you're telling yourself that says you have to live in it forever, isn't. The one that says you're damaged goods or full of baggage is a damn lie and that's the key: to find the lie, to find all the lies and rip them out like weeds. Bring them to the surface, pull them from their roots, and clear space for the truth to grow. You deserve to love and be loved.

You deserve to experience intimacy and pleasure and whatever the hell else you want for your life. It's time to break down those walls you've built up around yourself, strap on your combat boots, and conquer the greatest challenge of your life: the one within yourself. Unpack the bag, my friend. Dump it all out on the ground in front of you and get to work. All you have to lose is your excuses and your bullshit, but what you have to gain is love. Love like a flood, roaring like the rapids and gushing out of you conquering every lie the world tries to tell you about yourself in its path. You were created perfect, just as are you. Now it's time to rediscover who that person is and to set her free.

Shields up.
Shields down.
Shields shattered.

ACKNOWLEDGEMENTS

IT'S IMPOSSIBLE TO BEGIN THIS PAGE WITHOUT A STORY, SO here we go. I was standing in my kitchen reheating my coffee cup for the third time when a message shoved its way into my brain that shook me to my core: *You've got to write a book about sex.* The moment after, I literally said out loud to myself, "Well that's the craziest thing you've ever thought, Dre!" (Dre is how I refer to myself when no one is around). I let it go and went about my business but the thought kept finding its way back into my brain, growing louder each time. Almost a year after it first found its way into my mind, on February 6, 2018, I finally agreed to causally jot down what a book like that may look like, you know, just to get the voice off my back already. I had no idea that when I said "yes" to writing this book I was actually saying "yes" to taking back my life. Writing this story has changed my entire world in such profound ways and I'm so glad I didn't let the fear of these big topics keep me from uncovering the messages I found within these pages. This book looks nothing like I envisioned that February day, and I'm so grateful. I was just beginning what would become the most significant journey of my life to date, and I can't start these acknowledgements without thanking the person who gave me the freedom, wisdom, compassion, and unconditional love to do that: my husband, Derek Franklin.

Thank you Derek, for waking me up. You unknowingly lit a fire in my soul with those four little words and sent me on the greatest adventure. Thank you for loving me through the writing process which is a task I know wasn't always easy as I worked through big emotions that had been long tucked away. Thank you for pushing me to press on when I felt overwhelmed and for always being my biggest cheerleader in life, even when I say crazy things like, "I think I need to write a book about sex." Your love and support gave me the courage and strength I needed to pen these stories from my life and ours, and I'll never be able to express how grateful I am to you for that and for giving me permission to share some of our intimacy with others. I love you, far longer.

Thank you to my best friend, Alwyn Kanner, for being my soundboard. You saved this book before it started by nudging me to dig deeper. If it weren't for you, I may still be walking around with a heavy ass suitcase full of bullshit that's only half unpacked. Thank you for letting me run ideas off of you and for reading my work not only through the lens of my friend, but through the eyes of a writer. I love you, bequest.

Thank you to my grassroots beta readers and editors, Chrissy Pekema and Lindsay Houser. I was hot off the press with a first draft and you both took time out of your crazy schedules (hi, super moms!) to offer your brilliant thoughts and skills to this book, and I am so insanely grateful. This book would not be the same without you ladies.

Thank you to my editor, Stacy Shaneyfelt, for your attention to detail and creative input. You helped me polish the heck out of this bad boy and fixed all the ugly bits (of which there were many). Thank you to my cover and interior designer, Dania Zafar, for brining my vision to life.

Thank you to my children, Declan and Bennett, for bringing light into my darkest corners. It isn't your job, but you've saved me all the same. So much heartache has engulfed us in your short time on this earth, yet you both manage to act as beacons of sunlight amidst even the harshest storms.

Thank you, Brian Membrino, for inviting me into your family and teaching me what it means to truly live. I'll miss you always and carry our memories with me. Thank you, Kaiti Petsche, for being my sister by choice. I promise to continue to honor your life by being honest about who you were and who you weren't. You always wanted to be seen, and I'll use our story to keep your memory alive and help others, just like you would have wanted. I love you.

Thank you, mom and dad, for letting me express myself as a child so that I could express myself as an adult. Many parents have tried to tame a soul like mine, but you always let me stay wild and I love you for that.

Lastly, thank you to everyone in this book who helped make me who I am. Whether we shared happy memories or not, I'll take the lessons I've learned from our encounters with me for the rest of my days. It's been a true gift to unpack these events and move forward with love. I wish you well on your journey and hope you too, find the love you've been searching for. The love that already exists inside of you.

NOTES

INTRODUCTION: OPENING QUOTE

"Quote by Betty Friedan", Goodreads, accessed January 20, 2020, https://www.goodreads.com/quotes/1314

CHAPTER ONE: OPENING QUOTE

"Moliere Quotes", Goodreads, accessed January 19, 2020, https://www.goodreads.com/quotes/188304

CHAPTER TWO: OPENING QUOTE

"Quotes by Brian A. McBride" from *Dominion,* Goodreads, accessed January 20, 2020, https://www.goodreads.com/quotes/7098654

CHAPTER TWO: ABANDONMENT

1. R. Taverner, *Proverbs or Adages out of Erasmus* (1539), Merriam-Webster, accessed March 16, 2018, https://www.merriam-webster.com/dictionary/better%20the%20devil%20you%20know%20than%20the%20devil%20you%20don%27t

CHAPTER THREE: OPENING QUOTE

"Quotes by Carl Gustav Jung", Goodreads, accessed January 18, 2020, https://www.goodreads.com/quotes/347602

CHAPTER THREE: SHAME

Brown, Brene. "The Power of Vulnerability." TED. June, 2010. Lecture. Accessed on May 7, 2018, https://www.ted.com/talks/brene_brown_the_power_of_vulnerability

CHAPTER FOUR: OPENING QUOTE

"Fred Rogers Quotes", Goodreads, accessed January 20, 2020, https://www.goodreads.com/quotes/157666

CHAPTER FIVE: OPENING QUOTE

"Quotes by John Steinbeck", Goodreads, accessed on January 19, 2020, https://www.goodreads.com/quotes/77631

CHAPTER SIX: OPENING QUOTE

"Oprah Winfrey Quotes", Goodreads, accessed on January 19, 2020, https://www.goodreads.com/quotes/374257

CHAPTER SIX: REJECTION

1. "Mahatma Gandhi Quotes", Brainy Quote, accessed on April 27, 2018, https://www.brainyquote.com/quotes/mahatma_gandhi_109079
2. "Benedict Cumberbatch Quotes", Brainy Quote, accessed on April 27, 2018, https://www.brainyquote.com/quotes/benedict_cumberbatch_551349

CHAPTER SEVEN: OPENING QUOTE

"Brené Brown Quotes", *The Gifts of Imperfection (2010)*, Goodreads, accessed on January 21, 2020, https://www.goodreads.com/quotes/417396

CHAPTER EIGHT: OPENING QUOTE

"Mark Twain Quotes", Goodreads, accessed on January 21, 2020, https://www.goodreads.com/quotes/548857

CHAPTER NINE: OPENING QUOTE

"Quotes by Simone de Beauvoir", Goodreads, accessed on January 21, 2020, https://www.goodreads.com/quotes/407805

CHAPTER NINE: BODY-IMAGE

1. Mayo Clinic. (n.d.). Body Dysmorphic Disorder. Accessed on January 23, 2020, https://www.mayoclinic.org/diseases-conditions/body-dysmorphic-disorder/symptoms-causes/syc-20353938

2. Business Wire. 2019. The $72 Billion Weight Loss & Diet Control Market in the United States, 2019-2023 - Why Meal Replacements are Still Booming, but Not OTC Diet Pills - ResearchAndMarkets.com https://www.businesswire.com/news/home/20190225005455/en/72-Billion-Weight-Loss-Diet-Control-Market

CHAPTER TEN: OPENING QUOTE

"Alain de Botton Quotes", Goodreads, accessed on January 23, 2020, https://www.goodreads.com/quotes/538989

CHAPTER ELEVEN: OPENING QUOTE

Rowling, J.K.. *Harry Potter and the Order of the Phoenix.* (2003). Accessed from Goodreads on January 23, 2020, https://www.goodreads.com/quotes/63603

CHAPTER ELEVEN: GRIEF

Thomas, E. & Nolan, C. (2010). *Inception* [Motion Picture]. United States: Warner Bros. Pictures.

CHAPTER TWELVE: OPENING QUOTE

"Maya Angelou Quotes", Goodreads, accessed on January 20, 2020, https://www.goodreads.com/quotes/41814

CHAPTER THIRTEEN: OPENING QUOTE

"Anne Lamott Quotes", Goodreads, accessed on January 21, 2020, https://www.goodreads.com/quotes/39817

CHAPTER THIRTEEN: GRUDGES

"Reinhold Niebuhr Quotes", Brainy Quote, accessed on July 24, 2018, https://www.brainyquote.com/quotes/reinhold_niebuhr_121403

CHAPTER FOURTEEN: OPENING QUOTE

"Shannon L. Alder Quotes", Goodreads, accessed on January 23, 2020, https://www.goodreads.com/quotes/760778

CHAPTER FOURTEEN: SELF-WORTH

1. "Nayyirah Waheed Quote", Growth and Healing Wellness Center, accessed on November 22, 2018, https://growandheal.com/thought-of-the-day/

ABOUT THE AUTHOR

There isn't much left on the plate to tell about Andi Franklin after this unbarred and candid peek into her life. But for kicks, here we go:

Andi helps women reevaluate their experiences to find love, confidence, and joy within themselves. Her goal is to help them release their stories, grudges, insecurities, and shame so they can go out into the world and be the best, most kick ass version of themselves possible. Because healed people, can heal the world.

She doesn't eat ugly, pointy, or crunchy French fries.

She is pursuing her bachelor's degree in Psychology at Capella University.

When she isn't writing, you can find her speaking at women's conferences, playing board games with her kids, and Netflix binging with her husband, Derek.

Stay connected on social media:

- © instagram.com/andimariefranklin
- f facebook.com/imandifranklin
- ♫ twitter.com/andimfranklin

9 781734 612004